Knitting for Kittens

Knitting for Kittens

Learn to Loom Knit by Making 25 Cat Toys

by Darcy Oordt

Dedication

This book is dedicated to all those who devote their lives to helping rescue animals, especially those at Homeward Bound Pet Adoption Center located in Camden County, New Jersey.

Special thanks goes to Carolyn Fitzgerald and Maggie Moore, two wonderful friends that kept me sane and offered me the sound praise and criticism that I always needed to hear, even when I didn't want to hear it. Without them, this book would not be possible.

Acknowledgments

All kittens photographed for this book are courtesy of Homeward Bound Adoption Center's foster program. Homeward Bound is an animal shelter located in Camden County, New Jersey. The black cat is Minx, who allows the author, Darcy, to live with her and care for her needs.

About the Author

Darcy Oordt is a avid crafter who decided to use her love of cats and loom knitting into one book. She accepts that most would consider her a "crazy cat lady" but it's crazy with a purpose. For the past few years, she has worked to support her local animal shelters and is constantly fostering cats or kittens with severe medical needs. She currently resides in southern New Jersey. To find out more, check out her website, knittingforkittens.com.

First Edition

Design and Photography by Darcy Oordt

ISBN 978-1-7346289-4-4 (paperback)
ISBN 978-1-7346289-9-9 (ebook)

Published by Darcy Oordt Books
knittingforkittens.com

Table of Contents

Getting Started

This first section is meant to be an introduction to loom knitting cat toys. You won't learn everything about how to loom knit, only what you need to know to do the projects in this book.

Other than this book, the only things you need to get started is a12-peg loom, a loom hook, a tapestry needle, a skein of bulky or super bulky yarn, and a pair of scissors. Everything else is optional.

Loom Knitting Basics

Knitting is the art of interconnecting loops of yarn to create fabric. Needle knitting, the more familiar version, is done with two long needles. In contrast, loom knitting uses a loom and a hook. Loom knitting isn't new. As far as we know, it's as old as needle knitting.

This section is for those of you who have never loom knitted before. It will walk you through the basics of what you need to know before you get started. Don't worry if you've never knitted before. It's not as hard as you might imagine. If you are an experienced loom knitter, it's okay to gloss over this section. Although, checking out the section on numbering your loom makes the instructions easier to follow.

What is a loom?

A loom is simply a frame with a row of pegs on it. Looms come in a wide variety of shapes and sizes. For all the toys in this book you need the 12-peg loom, often referred to as a "flower loom." The loom measure about 4-inches in diameter and has 12 pegs around the top. On the side, is an anchor peg.

Loom knitting is done by creating a series of loops onto the loom. Instead of two needles, you create knit stitches with the loom and a device called a loom hook.

What else do you need?

To make the toys in this book, you need a 12-peg flower loom, a pair of scissors, a loom hook and a ball of yarn. Any additional items that are optional will be listed at the beginning of the toy. Hooks, needles, and scissors are easy to misplace, so I recommend that you have spares of each of these. Also, if you plan on doing a lot of knitting, ergonomic hooks such as the one sold by Authentic Knitting Board are worth the extra expense.

One last thing that is needed is super glue (cyanoacrylates). Adding a tip of super glue to the knots prevents them from loosening or unraveling. The type with the brush applicator allows you to apply it where you want it without getting it over everything.

How many rows?

If you are an experienced knitter, you may notice that instead of stating how many rows you should knit, the instructions list how long a piece should be. Trying to keep count of how many rows you've knitted can be tedious and frustrating, and for most of these toys, it won't matter. It also doesn't matter if you knit 1 inch or 1.5 inches, so don't feel you need a ruler on hand to measure your knitting. It's meant to be a guide, not a strict rule.

Understanding Yarn

Go into any yarn section of a craft store, and you will quickly be overwhelmed by the different types of yarn. You could spend an hour looking at it all and never pick up the same yarn twice. When looking for yarn for cat toys, you need to focus on a few things:

Weight: Yarn is categorized by its weight. Rather than go into all the details that determine a yarn's weight, let's go over what you need to know now. It is recommended that you use either super bulky or bulky yarn. A yarn's weights is identified with a symbol that looks like a skein of yarn with a number inside it. Eventually, you will be able to use lighter yarns by doubling them up or combining them with other yarns (which is covered later in "Multiple Strands" on page 99.

Care Instructions: I recommend finding a yarn that is machine washable. While many of the toys will wear out before they need washing, it's nice to be able to wash them when needed. Also, yarn that is durable enough to be machine washed should be durable enough for any cat.

Strength: Be sure to test the strength of the yarn by pulling on it to see if it breaks. I used to believe that any yarn labeled for babies would be a good fit for cats. However, while making a toy with "baby" yarn, I pulled too hard and the yarn snapped on me. I immediately threw the toy and the yarn away. Since then, I recommend pulling on the yarn to test its strength before using it to make a toy.

Color: Cats only see blues, grays and possibly yellows and greens. When choosing colors, realize that you are choosing them for you, not your cat.

How much yarn?

None of the toys indicate how much yarn is needed because they don't require that much. If you near the end of a skein of yarn, you might run out of yarn. But it really shouldn't be an issue that comes up. Moreover, the reality is that it would be impossible for you to determine how much yardage is left in a skein of yarn unless you unraveled and measured it. And nobody has time for that.

Numbering your Loom and Right- vs. Left-Handed Knitting

For clarity in the instructions, I encourage you to number the pegs of your loom with a permanent marker. Because I am right-handed, my loom is numbered clockwise. Peg 1 is the first peg to the left of the anchor peg and Peg 12 is the first peg to the right hand. This allows me to hold the working yarn in my left hand and keep my loom hook in my right. When I work in the round, I knit clockwise around the loom.

However, if you are left-handed, you can switch it around and knit counterclockwise. The piece will end up the same. Do whatever feels most comfortable to you. Remember that if you choose to knit counterclockwise, you will need to reverse directional words in the instruction such as "clockwise" and "counterclockwise."

Terms You Need to Know

While there is a more extensive glossary in the back, there are a few terms that you need to know before getting started.

A **Loom** is a frame with pegs placed evenly apart that you use to "knit." Most looms have an **Anchor Peg** on the side of the loom that is often used to secure, or "anchor," the yarn before you start a project.

The **Loom Hook** is used to help loop the yarn to create the stitch. They usually come with any loom you purchase but can be bought separately.

A **Yarn or Tapestry Needle** is a large, blunt needle usually made out of plastic. Both the Square and mouse require a yarn needle to help you close the ends. But it can also be used to help tuck the tail into the piece. I recommend purchasing a few extra of these as they are easy to lose or misplace.

A **Stitch** is the process of wrapping and looping the yarn.

A **Loop** is the yarn wrapped around the peg. The **Existing Loop** is the loop of yarn on the peg. This loop is used to loop over the new loop to create a stitch. The **New Loop** is the loop on the peg created with the working yarn that hasn't been knitted yet.

The **Tail** is the yarn that is not part of the knitting. When it is at the beginning, it is known as the **Starting Tail**. When it is at the end of a piece, it is the **Ending Tail.** It is the yarn after the last knit stitch.

The **Working Yarn** that comes from the ball. It's the yarn you are "working" with as opposed to the tail.

A **Row** is a series of stitches between two pegs on the loom.

A **Skein of Yarn** is a unit of yarn. Units of yarn have terms based on the shape they form after they are wound. A "ball" of yarn is wound in a circle or ball shape, which is usually done by hand-winding it. Most yarns are sold in skeins, which is an oblong shape. For this reason, a skein of yarn is also used to mean any unit of yarn. Other yarn forms include cake, hank, cone, and donut. In this book, skein or ball is used to refer as the basic unit of yarn.

No Abbreviations

This book does not use abbreviations. When I was working on this book, I took the time to look at

criticism of other loom knitting books. I saw many complaints about the use of abbreviations. Abbreviations have their place, and I understand why the authors chose to use them.

This book assumes that you likely have no loom knitting experience, so abbreviations are not used. I also tend to give detailed instructions, partially based on my frustration with directions when I was beginning and because I have a degree in education.

Loom Knitting Cat Toys

When you knit a hat or scarf, you usually don't worry about how it's going to hold up under a daily attack of teeth and claws. To keep your cat safe, you need to understand techniques for loom knitting cat toys that don't necessarily apply to other knitting projects.

I've thoroughly tested these toys with my cats and numerous foster cats and kittens in my care. The test process involved watching them carefully as they played with the toys and checking the toys for any damage. I urge you to do routinely the same thing. Supervise your cat with any new toys you give them before considering them safe. Do this with all toys, including the ones your purchase.

The strength and durability of these toys will vary depending on your skill, the type of yarn used and on the cat. Some cats are more aggressive and destructive with their toys than others. Cat toys are something that should bring joy, not pain to you and your cat's life. For this reason, I've compiled a list of guidelines that I urge you to read and follow.

Secure the Cat Toys.

I read somewhere that "True knitting doesn't contain knots." However, cat knitting — or rather knitting cat toys — require knots. If you come across other methods of dealing with the tail (such as weaving it into the fabric), please disregard them when making toys.

Securing the ends of your knitting with knots is not an option. It's a requirement to ensure the toy doesn't unravel. The knots are for your cat's safety.

Also, secure all the knots with super glue. I've had knots loosen on me when I haven't taken this step. Buy the super glue that comes with a brush applicator as it makes applying the glue easier than if it is in a tube.

Be Attentive When Introducing New Toys to Your Cat.

There's no way around this one. You need to supervise your cat with the toys at first. While none of the toys have ever caused any harm or even danger, it is better to be safe than sorry.

The biggest concern is the yarn might break or embellishments aren't attached securely and come off. Most yarn won't break easily. However, you should test it before making any toys. One yarn purchased during the writing of this book snapped during a toy's construction. And, it wasn't just a weak point in that particular yarn.

Test Your Toys' Durability First.

The best way to test how durable your toys are is to throw them into your washing machine during a normal cycle. If they don't unravel during this process, you're securing the ends properly. If the toy unravels, then you need to add an extra knot or use a bit more glue.

The washing machine test should also help ensure the yarn is durable enough. Once you are adept at making the toys and familiar with your materials, you won't have to keep washing them. But it's the most thorough way to figure out how secure your knitting is and if it will endure your cat.

Contain Your Yarn.

Keep your yarn in a safe and secure place when not in use. Most craft stores sell yarn storage devices you can use. I have tried a variety of them and usually use one of two items: small craft bags or plastic food containers.

The small craft bags are big enough to hold several balls of yarn, a loom, scissors, and a loom hook plus anything else I might want. Plus, they are easy to take with me to appointments and are usually cheap to purchase.

When I need to protect my yarn I'm using from adventurous kittens, I like to use large disposable plastic food containers. Cut a small notch out of the rim of the bottom. When knitting, the hole allows you to use the yarn with the lid closed. When you stop knitting, you can store your loom, loom hook and scissors inside with your yarn. (If you cut a hole in the lid, you won't be able to use the container to hold your loom while you are in the middle of a project.

Some Toys Always Require Supervision.

Toys like the door hangers should always be supervised as there is a risk your cat could get entangled and strangle themselves. I recommend that you put the toy away at night or when you're away from home. Not only will this protect your cat, but it will make the toy more special.

It's also a good idea to create door hangers that hang several inches off the floor. The lowest they should be is at eye level to your cat when he is sitting, if not higher. Cats enjoy reaching up to grab things. Keep in mind that the yarn may stretch slightly as your cat plays with it, so you may need to adjust the height.

Balls of Yarn are Not Toys.

Despite the numerous images of cats cheerfully playing with balls of yarn, they are not toys. Yarn is deadly. The loose yarn could get wrapped around your cat and strangle him or her. Yarn can also be deadly if your cat ingests it.

Call Your Vet Immediately if Your Cat Ingest Any Part of a Toy.

If you suspect your cat has eaten any yarn or part of a toy, contact a vet immediately. If you find yarn in your cat's mouth, you can try to pull it out gently, but stop if you run into any resistance. If you don't stop, you could cause damage to your cat's internal organs. Even if you feel you've removed the yarn, you should contact your vet for further instructions and advice.

Throw Away Worn Out Toys.

These toys are not designed to last forever. When they start to get worn out, toss them. Usually, yarn will start to fuzz rather than fray, which is more about the appearance of a toy than its durability.

Embellishments

Embellishments include anything that is added to the toy that isn't part of the original knitting. When I first started making these toys, I didn't intend to include any embellishments. All of the toys were created from one skein of yarn. But I realized that cat toys needed to appeal to both cats and people. (To be honest, that was something a friend said to me. And she was right.)

Embellishments are covered at the end of the book. Although I only include options that I have found safe, I encourage you to use caution and your own best judgment.

Knit Stitches

Knitting has two types of stitches: knit and purl. Knit stitches create a V pattern on the right side of the fabric. The purl stitch creates a line pattern on the outside side of the fabric, with the V pattern being on the inside side of the fabric. Although the knit stitch is one type of stitch, loom knitting has four different ways of creating it: e-wrap, u-wrap, flat, and true or traditional.

One of the most significant differences between the four methods is their tightness or tension. Tension will affect the size, density, and feel of your knitting. When you have more tension in your stitches, the piece you create is smaller and the fabric is denser and stiffer.

Flat knit produces the tightest knit. The stitches are closer together and create a smaller piece of fabric. On the other end of the spectrum is the e-wrap. The four balls pictured here were all created on the same loom with the same yarn and precisely 10 rows of stitches. Although separately shown, they were photographed together and none of the images have been resized. As you can see, the flat knit ball is the smallest.

Flat Knit

U-Wrap and true knit are both in the middle. In the photo, u-wrap looks tighter than the true knit. However, that's more about how I knit than about the stitch itself. I naturally like to pull the u-wrap tight against the peg, which creates a tighter knit.

U-Wrap Knit

However, when I don't pull on the working yarn so much, I create a stitch that looks like the true knit version.

For beginners and younger children, I recommend starting with the e-wrap stitches. It's the easiest of all of them to maneuver, and it won't get too tight if it's not done right. I like the u-wrap stitch and use it almost exclusively. It looks just like the true knit stitch but is a lot easier to do.

Please note that some people also refer to stitch patterns as "stitches." Knit stitch patterns are made using knit and purl stitches to create a design in the fabric. For example, the garter stitch pattern is made by alternating rows of knit and purl stitches. This book does not cover stitch patterns. If you are interested, I will put some on my website knittingforkittens.com.

True Knit

E-Wrap Knit

E-Wrap Knit Stitch (Twisted Knit Stitch)

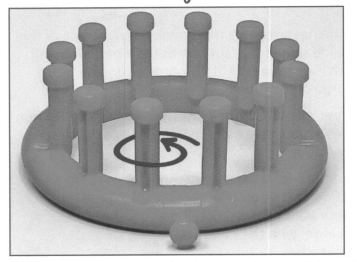

The e-wrap knit stitch is so-called because it is created by wrapping the yarn behind the peg, around the front and then behind it again. Much the same way you'd make a cursive lowercase "e" with the top of the e being in front of the peg.

It is also referred to as the "twisted knit stitch" because of its appearance. Instead of the regular V pattern associated with knitting, it creates a Y shape that overlaps slightly. Instead of a straight stitch, it appears slightly twisted.

The e-wrap has the benefit of being faster than other knit stitches because you can wrap several pegs at one time before pausing to knit over.

Also, because you completely wrap the peg, it is difficult to slip a stitch. Slipping a stitch is when you remove the loop on the peg without attaching a new loop. The ease of this stitch makes it an excellent choice for beginners and younger children.

One major drawback to using this stitch is the lack of tension in the fabric. When stuffed, the pattern expands, which creates small holes, showing the "insides" of the toy. The other major drawback is that it doesn't look like traditional knitting as the rows are not straight.

Up close it is easy to see the difference between the e-wrap stitch (left) and the u-wrap stitch (right). U-Wrap, Flat and True knit stitches all create the same look.

U-Wrap Knit Stitch

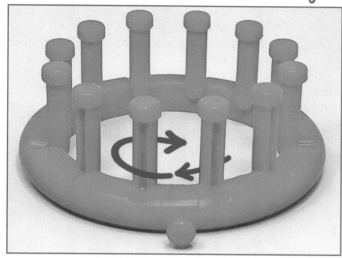

The u-wrap knit stitch's name also comes from the way you wrap the yarn around the peg. To create it, you wrap the yarn around the front of the peg and to the back (so the working yarn will end up next to the peg last knitted). In other words, you create a sideways U around the peg.

This stitch has a lot of advantages to it. First, it creates the traditional V pattern associated with knitting. Second, it is easy to do and, with practice, becomes almost as quick as the e-wrap knit stitch. Third, you easily can control the tightness of the stitches by how tightly you hold the yarn to the peg.

Tightly knit fabric is denser with less flexibility to it. While it may seem like you should hold the working yarn tightly against the peg, it's not necessary and can make it difficult to knit the next row because the existing loops don't have any give to them.

For your best results, hold the yarn, so it is just barely against the peg. When you do that, you will create a stitch that closely resembles the true knit stitch.

Flat Knit Stitch

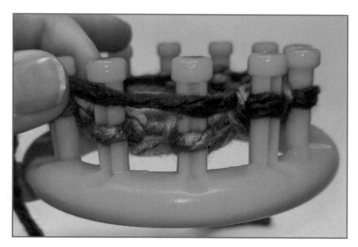

The flat knit stitch is so named because the yarn is held flat against the front of the peg, instead of going around the peg.

The flat knit stitch is the tightest knit but also the most difficult. The problem I have with it is that when knitting over, the working yarn can end up going with the loop, which means you must stop and fix it. This is known as "slipping" a stitch. To reduce the chances of this, try holding the working yarn just behind the next peg instead of in front of it.

Unless you need to create a tightly knitted fabric, you won't find a need to use this stitch. While it might seem quicker than the u-wrap knit stitch, it's too easy to slip stitches, which is a headache to fix.

True, Traditional, or Classic Knit Stitch

The true knit stitch is also called the traditional or classic knit stitch. It gets its name because many believe it is the closest to what is produced through needle knitting. However, it takes more work to create this stitch than any of the others. However, it is extremely close in appearance to the u-wrap knit stitch.

Step 1: Hold the yarn flat against the peg above the existing loop.

Step 2: Take your hook from under the loop and snag the working yarn.

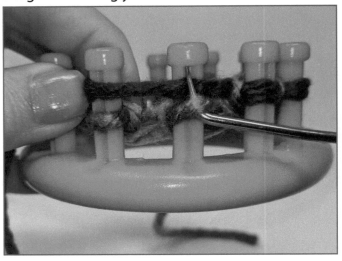

Step 3: Pull the working yarn down underneath the loop and out to make a new loop that extends out from the loop on the peg.

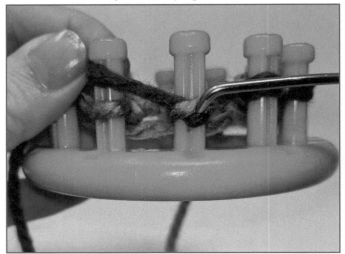

Step 4: While holding the new loop, lift the existing loop from the peg and replace it with the new loop.

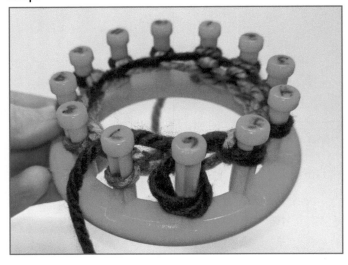

Step 5: Pull the working yarn to tighten the loop.

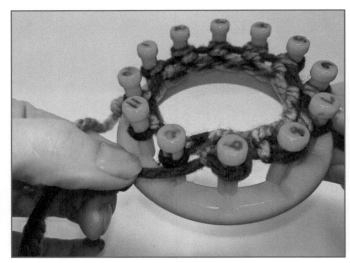

Purl Stitch

The purl stitch is the opposite of a knit stitch because it creates the V-shaped pattern on the inside of the fabric, instead of the outside. And it is done just like the true knit stitch except the yarn is placed below the existing loop (instead of above).

Step 1: Hold the yarn flat against the peg below the existing loop.

Step 2: Take your hook from above the loop and snag the working yarn.

Step 4: While holding the new loop, lift the existing loop from the peg and replace it with the new loop.

Step 3: Pull the working yarn up and make a new loop that extends out from the loop on the peg.

Step 5: Pull the working yarn to tighten the loop.

Adding a row or two of purl stitches onto a toy is a simple way of creating texture and make it more visually interesting.

How to Tie a Slip Knot

Before you can learn how to loom knit, you must learn how to tie a slip knot. You use it to attach the yarn to one of the pegs or the anchor pegs before you begin knitting. It is used at the start of every toy.

Step 1: Put your middle and index fingers of your left hand together. With your left thumb, hold the end of the yarn against your fingers. If you want a long string to use to tie the toy, your thumb should be holding the yarn about 4 inches from the end.

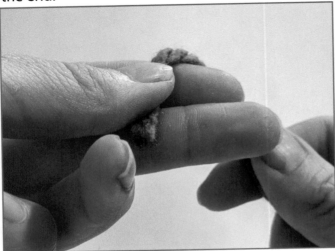

Step 2: With your right hand, wrap the yarn around your fingers. Then, push the yarn in your hand underneath the circle of yarn on your fingers, in-between your index and middle fingers. Make a small loop.

Step 3: Pull your fingers out of the circle holding onto the loop. Grasping the loop in one hand and the two ends in the other, gently pull to tighten the knot.

Step 4: Place the loop around a peg (usually the anchor peg), pull the two ends to tighten it.

Understanding the Patterns

Before the instructions for each toy you will find information that will tell you what to expect and what you will need. These are organized under the following sections. If a section is not included in the toy's introduction, it means that it wasn't necessary.

Skill Level: Toys are categorized into four different skill levels: Beginner, Developing, Practiced, Proficient. Beginner toys are the base toys that teach many of the skills. Developing and Practiced are more advanced and will require one or more skills learned with a previous toy. Proficient are the hardest toys to make.

Skills Learned: Rather than list the instructions for the skills in a separate section, they are included within the instructions for the first toy they are used. To highlight this, I will note which skills you will learn when making the toy.

Skills Required: If the toy uses a skill that is taught elsewhere, it will list it here. It is recommended that you learn the skill by making the toy it is taught first.

Time to Make: This is just an estimation of how long it may take you to make each toy.

Finished Size: Approximate size of the toy once it is completed. Of course, size will vary on many of them depending on how many rows you knit.

Materials Required: If the toy requires anything besides a loom and yarn to complete, it will be listed here.

Suggested Embellishments: Suggestions on what embellishments you might want to consider trying once you have mastered making the toy.

Pattern Notes: Anything else I wanted to say that didn't fit into the above sections.

Making Toys

You've got the yarn. You've got the loom. You are ready to make your first toy. If you're new to knitting, the toys at the front will teach you the skills necessary to make the more advanced toys.

Basic Ball

The Basic Ball was the first toy I made with the 12-peg loom. It essentially started this whole book. It is a good choice for practicing color changes and stitch patterns because the cast on is quick. If you make a mistake or don't like the outcome, you don't have a lot of time invested in your work.

Skill Level:
Beginner

Skills Learned:
Drawstring Cast On (p. 24), Gathered Removal Bind Off (p. 25)

Skills Required:
Any Knit Stitch (p. 13)

Time to Make:
15 minutes

Finished Size:
1.5 to 2.5 inches

Materials Required:
Stuffing (p. 26)

Suggested Embellishments:
Beads (p. 96), Fuzzy Yarn (p. 99), Multiple Strands (p. 99), Stitch Patterns (p. 98), Switching Colors (p. 100), Catnip (p. 98)

Pattern Notes:
The Ball will teach you the Drawstring Cast On and the Gathered Removal Bind Off. These two skills are used frequently and serve as the foundation for more complex toys like the Snark (p. 61) and the Octopus (p. 64). The balls pictured above were all done with the u-wrap knit stitch (p. 15).

Step 1: Cast on with the Drawstring Cast On (p. 24).

Step 2: Knit in the round until it is about 1-1/2 inches long (about 10 to 15 rows).

Step 3: Finish with the Gathered Removal Bind Off (p. 25).

Step 4: When you are finished, stretch out the piece to even out the stitches. Pull on the piece in every direction. Stretching will even out the stitches and give the piece a more uniform look.

Step 5: Turn the piece inside out and gently pull on one of the strings to close the end. You will get a better close if you find the "drawstring" underneath the loops and tug at it gently in several places rather than trying to close it by pulling on the end.

Step 6: Tie a secure knot. Trim the tail so it is about 2 inches long.

Step 7: Reverse the ball so it is right-side out.

Step 8: Stuff the ball as desired (p. 26).

Step 9: Pull on the remaining drawstring to close the other end. When done, secure it with a knot.

Step 10: Tuck the end into the piece through the hole. If necessary, you can thread the end through an embroidery needle. Then push it through the side and trim off any excess yarn.

Drawstring Cast On

The Drawstring Cast On is designed so the end can be closed by pulling on the starting tail. It is used for the **Ball** (p. 22), **Ladybug** (p. 28), **1-Tailed Ball** (p. 55), **2-Tailed Ball** (p. 58), **Snark** (p. 61), **Octopus** (p. 64), **Ball Door Hanger** (p. 73), and **Mouse** (p. 82).

Step 1: Tie a slip knot and place it on the anchor peg.

Step 2: Loop the yarn around the back of the Peg 1 and then around to the front of Peg 2.

Step 2: Continue weaving the yarn around the rest of the pegs alternating between going behind the odd-numbered pegs and in front of the even-numbered pegs.

Step 3: When back at the start, go behind Peg 1 a second time.

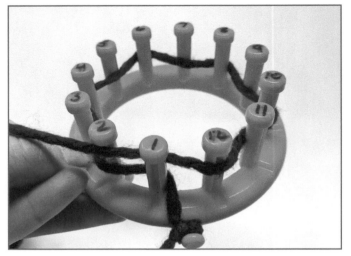

Step 4: Wrap the yarn around the loom, holding it tight against the front of the pegs. Whenever the yarn is in front of a peg with yarn with a loop below it, knit the bottom loop over the top loop. This will occur on the even numbered pegs.

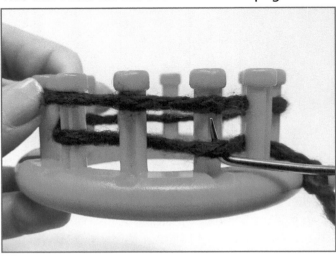

Step 5: Bring the yarn in front of Peg 1. You will start knitting with Peg 2.

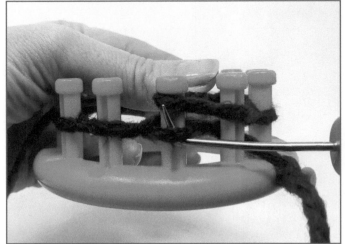

Gathered Removal Bind Off

Like the Drawstring Cast On, the Gathered Removal Bind Off is designed so you can close the end by pulling on the tail. It is used with most of the toys including the **Ball** (p. 22), **Ladybug** (p. 28), **1-Tailed Ball** (p. 55), **2-Tailed Ball** (p. 58), **Snark** (p. 61), **Octopus** (p. 64), **Ball Door Hanger** (p. 73), **Disc** (p. 74), **Spider** (p. 76), **Flower** (p. 79), and **Jellyfish** (p. 87).

Step 1: Wrap the working yarn about 1-1/2 times around the loom and cut it. Once you've mastered this skill, you can reduce this amount. But for now, it's better to have plenty of yarn to work with rather than too little..

Step 2: Hook your loom hook down through the top of the loop on Peg 1 and snag the working yarn. Twist your hook slightly and gently pull the yarn all the way through the loop.

Step 3: Repeat Step 2 on Peg 2. However, when you are finished, you can remove the loop from Peg 2. (Don't remove the loop from Peg 1 until after Step 5.)

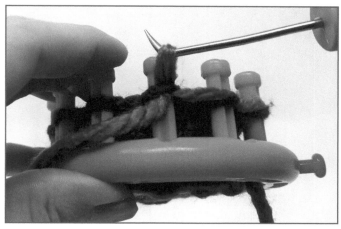

Step 4: Repeat Step 3 with pegs 3 – 12. Continue removing the loops from each peg.

Step 5: When you get back to Peg 1, pull the yarn through the loop a second time. You can now remove the loop from Peg 1.

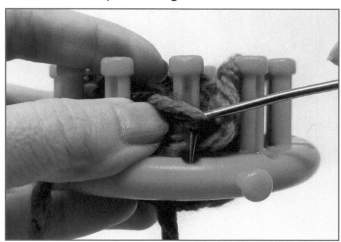

Stuffing Toys

Toys like the **Ball** (p. 22), **Square** (p. 30), and **Mouse** (p. 82) require stuffing. But don't feel like you have to purchase it. You can use materials found around the house. The following is just a few examples of things you can use. I recommend you trying them all and see which you (and your cat) likes best.

Plastic Bags

Grocery and other plastic shopping bags create a light-weight toy and help keep these bags out of landfills. As a bonus, the balls are washable and make a crinkly sound.

Polyfil Stuffing

Polyfil is the traditional choice for stuffing toys. It makes a ball that is squishy, soft, and even lighter than ones stuffed with plastic bags. And it's cheap because one bag will fill 2 or 3 toys.

Fabric

Use leftover bits of fabric such as clothing or sheets to stuff the toy. If you use a heavy material, such as denim, it will give the toy more weight which some cats prefer. Fabric also allows you to wash the toys.

Beans

Dried beans will create a more substantial toy that moves and reacts differently than balls made from the other materials. Bean-stuffed toys won't be washable. Also avoid using with toys created using the e-wrap knit stitch or with a knit pattern because the beans fall out.

Alternate Versions

Tired of soft, round balls? With a little adjustment, you can create one of these four toys. Most just require you to increase the number of rows in the ball. Each one has a different feel and movement to it, and you might be surprised to find your cat likes one of these better than the basic ball.

Ball Cover

If you're like me, you have an extensive collection of cheap plastic balls. They come in a lot of toy packages and seem to be the least favorite toy. They are also the perfect size to fit inside these knitted balls. It creates a firm ball that is lightweight.

Egg-selent Egg

If you shop right after Easter, you will find plastic eggs extremely cheap. To cover, knit a slightly larger ball than normal Before inserting the egg, place a couple of small rocks inside the egg to make them rattle and tape or glue it closed. If there is a small hole in the egg, you can also add a bit of catnip inside.

Toy-let Paper Tube

To make a slightly different toy, use part of an empty toilet or paper towel roll. When making this toy, don't tie off the ends until after you insert the tube. Tie each end until they are mostly closed. A small hole at each end will occur. You can even add a treat inside for extra fun.

Cat Kicker

Essentially, a cat kicker is simply a long ball. Keep knitting the ball until it is 4 inches long or more. To give it more weight, I stuff mine with old sheets or towels, but it's up to you. Use the e-knit stitch to make a wider cat kicker or the u-knit stitch if you want a narrower one.

Ladybug

My cat loves to bat these across my wood floor and then chase it down. But you don't need a smooth surface for your cat to enjoy tossing or carrying them around your home.

Skill Level:
Developing

Skills Required:
Drawstring Cast On (p. 24), Gathered Removal Bind Off (p. 25), Any Knit Stitch (p. 13)

Time to Make:
15 minutes

Finished Size:
1.5 to 2.5 inches

Materials Required:
Pipe Cleaner

Suggested Embellishments:
Felt (p. 96)

Pattern Notes:
You don't need to add the pipe cleaner antenna if you don't have one. If you are interested in using puffy paint like on the orange bug, check out instructions on my website, kittingforkittens.com.

Step 1: Follow the directions for the Ball but don't close either end (p. 22).

Step 2: Cut a pipe cleaner in half and fold it into a 45-degree angle. If one end was pointing at Peg 1 on your loom, the other end would be pointing at Peg 3.

Step 3: Close one end of the ball like normal.

Step 4: Turn the ball inside out.

Step 5: Gently insert one end of the pipe cleaner into the ball next to the closed hole. Then, insert the other end of the pipe cleaner into the knitted fabric on the other side of the closed hole.

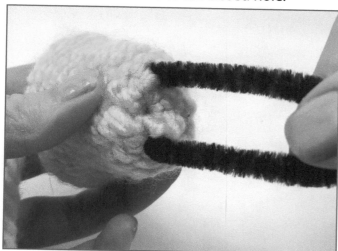

Step 6: Check the placement by inverting the ball slightly after you've inserted the pipe cleaner part way. If it's in the right place, move to the next step. If not, repeat Steps 5 & 6.

Step 7: Gently twist the bent piece of pipe cleaner to secure it.

Step 8: Invert the ball so it is right side is out.

Step 9: Close the other end of the ball.

Step 10: Shape the pipe cleaners to make the antennae.

Square Toy

The Square Toy is plain and simple, but one many cats seem to really enjoy. My cat Caffrey adores this toy above all others and I am frequently having to replace it because he's worn it out.

Skill Level:
Beginner

Skills Learned:
E-Wrap Cast On (p. 33), Basic Bind Off (p. 36)

Skills Required:
Any Knit Stitch (p. 13)

Time to Make:
40 minutes

Finished Size:
2 in. wide, length varies

Materials Required:
Stuffing (p. 26)

Suggested Embellishments:
Felt (p. 96), Multiple Strands (p. 99), Stitch Patterns (p. 98), Switching Colors (p. 100), Catnip (p. 98)

Pattern Notes:
The Square Toy is perfect for trying out new stitch patterns or color changes. And if you're good at cutting felt, you can make personalized toys for all your cats. I also recommend stuffing them with catnip because the size enables cats to rub their faces on them and enjoy it.

Step 1: Cast on with the E-Wrap Cast On leaving a 5-inch long tail (p. 33).

Step 2: Knit using any knit stitch until the piece is about 4 inches long.

Step 3: Finish with the Basic Bind Off (p. 36). Again, leave a 5-inch long tail.

Step 4: Gently stretch the knitting by pulling the pieces in all directions. This helps set the stitches.

Step 5: Turn the knitting inside out.

Step 6: You are now going to sew close the end that was casted on. You can tell it from the other end because it is loopier rather than a row of V's. Thread the tail for the cast on end through an embroidery needle and sew it closed. You don't need to use any fancy stitches. Just go back and forth through the top loops.

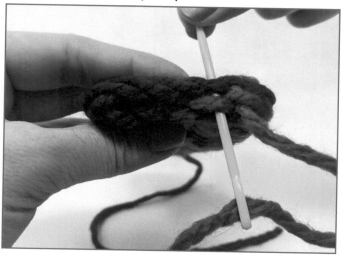

Step 7: When you get to the end, test that it is closed securely by pulling on the sides. If necessary, go back and forth through it again. Tie a knot as close to the fabric as you can.

Step 8: Turn the knitting so it is right side out.
Step 9: Stuff. See **Stuffing Toys** (p. 26).
Step 10: Repeat Steps 6 & 7 with the other end. Because the bind off end has a row of V's, move the needle in-between the V to close.

Step 11: After tying the knot, loop the tail through the embroidery needle again and sew it through the piece. Cut off any excess that yarn that protrudes from the toy.

E-Wrap Cast On (in the Round)

The E-Wrap Cast On (in the Round) can be used on any piece that will create a tube, instead of a flat piece. It's not the most elegant cast on out there, but its simple and does the job. Once you have learned the steps for this cast on, try the advanced version. This cast on is used with Square (p. 30), Milk Ring (p. 38), Disc (p. 74), Spider (p. 76), Flower & Hoop (p. 79).

Step 1: Tie a slip knot and place it on the anchor peg. For the Square, you should create the slip knot so it has a 5-inch tail. For other toys, you only need a tail that is 1 to 2 inches long.

Step 2: Going between Pegs 12 and 1, wrap the yarn counterclockwise around Peg 1. This is also known as e-wrapping a peg.

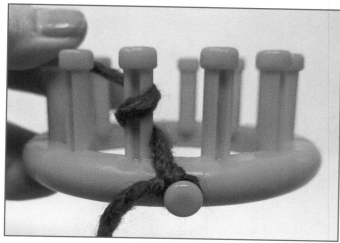

Step 3: E-Wrap the yarn counterclockwise around the rest of the pegs until you are back at Peg 1. Try to place the loop at least midway on the peg.

Step 4: E-Wrap Peg 1 above the first loop.

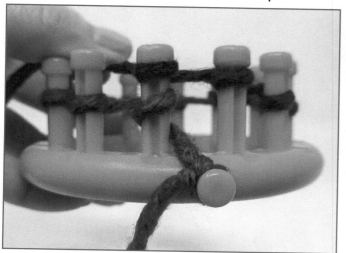

Step 5: Knit over the bottom loop of Peg 1 by pulling it over the top loop. This will prevent your first row from unraveling if you drop the yarn.

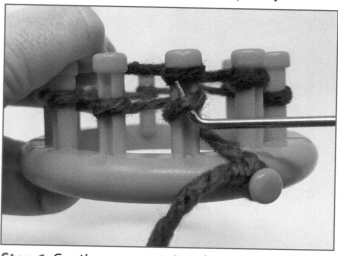

Step 6: Continue e-wrapping the remaining loops. If necessary, gently push down your first row to make room for the next row of e-wrap. If you have trouble keeping the yarn tight enough to keep it on the pegs, knit the pegs immediately after you wrap them. (Otherwise, wait.)

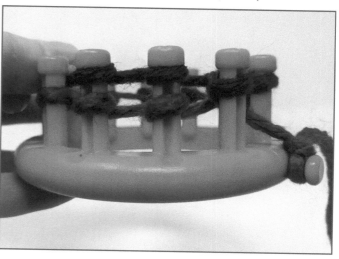

Step 7: When you reach Peg 12, knit the bottom loop over the top. This will hold the yarn in place.

Step 8: Knit Pegs 2 through 11. You are now ready to start knitting your rows of stitches.

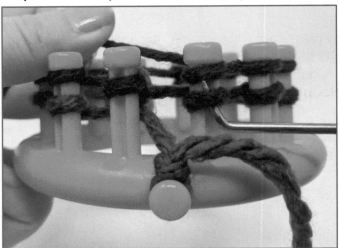

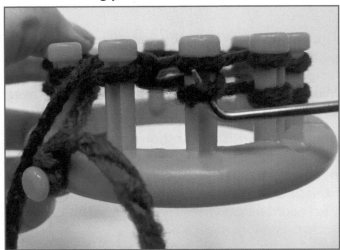

Advanced E-Wrap Cast On

The advanced method is tighter and neater than the regular method. It takes a little practice because you need to be able to hold the yarn taut while wrapping the loom twice. If you let loose too early, the entire thing will unravel and you have to start over. It can be used with the Square (p. 30), **Milk Ring** (p. 38), **Disc** (p. 74), or **Spider** (p. 76).

Step 1: Tie a slip knot and place it on the anchor peg. For a square, the tail should be 5 inches long; other toys can have a shorter tail.

Step 2: Going between Peg 12 and Peg 1, wrap the yarn counterclockwise around Peg 1. Repeat until all pegs are covered. The yarn should be midway on the peg. If not, push the loops down before you start the next step.

Step 3: E-Wrap the pegs again, with the 2nd loop resting above the 1st one. Stop when you have 2 loops on each peg.

Step 4: Knit Peg 12. You can now release the working yarn.

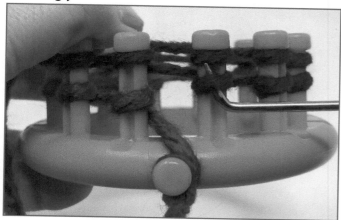

Step 5: Knit Peg 11. As you do so, tug on the bottom loop to tighten the yarn. This will create a bigger loop.

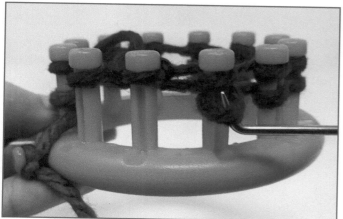

Step 6: Repeat Step 5 for the remaining pegs. The loop will get bigger as you work down the pegs. You will want to grasp the loop to keep the yarn tight as you go.

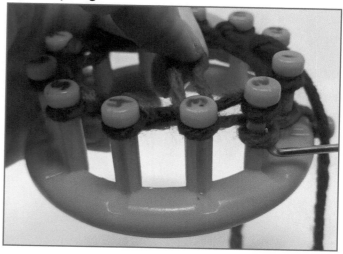

Step 7: When you get down to Peg 1, remove the slip knot (tail) from the anchor peg. Tug on the tail to tighten the cast on.

Step 8: Secure the tail back onto the anchor peg. As it can be challenging to create a slip knot in the right spot, tie a simple knot to keep it secure. Once you have done one row of knitting, you don't have to worry about it coming loose.

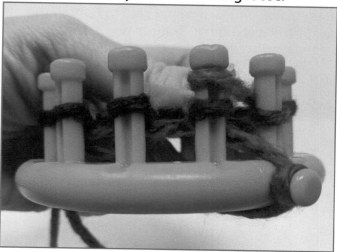

Basic Bind Off

The Basic Bind Off gives you a clean edge to your knitting piece. It is used with the **Square** (p. 30), **Milk Ring** (p. 38), and **Hoop** (p. 79).

Step 1: Knit Pegs 1 & 2.

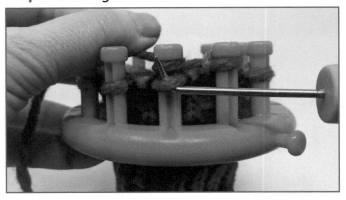

Step 2: Gently tug on the loop on the last knitted peg (Peg 2) to make it larger.

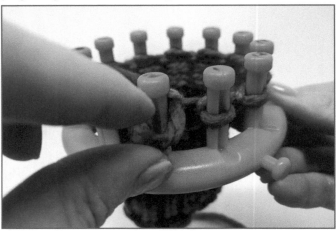

Step 3: Move the loop over to the previous peg (Peg 1). Pull on the working yarn to tighten the loop after it is moved. Knit the peg (Peg 1).

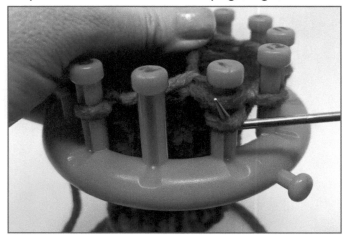

Step 4: Move the loop from the peg (Peg 1) back to the original peg (Peg 2). Peg 1 has now been "bound off."

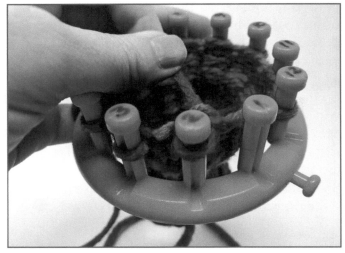

Step 5: Knit the next peg (Peg 3).

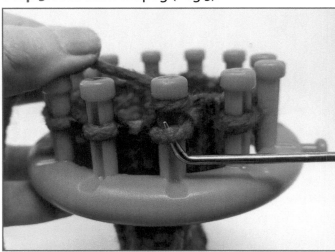

Step 6: Repeat Steps 2 – 5 with Pegs 2 and 3. (Add 1 to the Peg numbers to get the right peg numbers.)

Step 7: Repeat Steps 2 – 5 with the rest of the pegs until only two are left (Pegs 11 and 12). For clarity, you are going to knit one peg. Move it back to the first peg in the row. Knit. Then move the loop so it is back on its original peg next to the other pegs with loops.

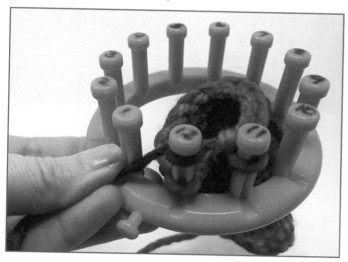

Step 8: Knit Peg 12 and move it over to Peg 11.
Step 9: Knit Peg 11.

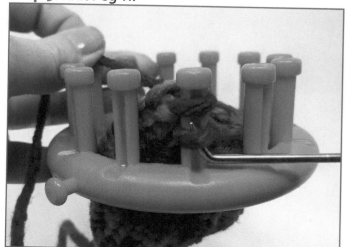

Step 10: Cut the working yarn leaving about a 5-inch tail for the Square toy. Other toys can have a shorter tail. Pull the tail through the remaining loop and pull it through.

Step 11: Remove the loop from the peg and pull on the tail to tighten it.

Oreo's Milk Ring

My cat Oreo loved the little plastic rings from the milk carton lids. After he passed away, I found a stash of them he had hidden away for a rainy day. Newer milk lids no longer have rings, which are bad for the environment. But thankfully, these are not and I hope your cats enjoy them as much as mine.

Skill Level:
Beginner

Skills Required:
E-Wrap Cast On (p. 33), Basic Bind Off (p. 36), Any Knit Stitch (p. 13)

Time to Make:
10 minutes

Finished Size:
2-by-2 inches

Suggested Embellishments:
Fringe (p. 97), Multiple Strands (p. 99), Fuzzy Yarn (p. 99)

Pattern Notes:
The Milk Ring is a fast way to teach and practice the E-Wrap Cast On and Basic Bind Off. The method of creating is the same as the Square with fewer rows, no stuffing and no sewing the ends closed.

Step 1: Cast on with the E-Wrap Cast On (p. 33).

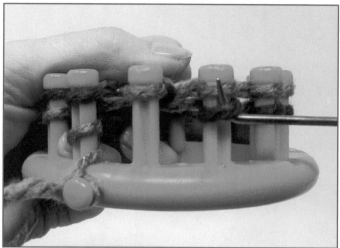

Step 3: Finish with the Basic Bind Off (p. 36).

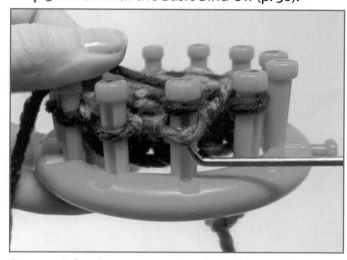

Step 2: Knit 3 or 4 rows. You can either continue e-wraping the pegs or, if you prefer, switch to the u-wrap knit stitch.

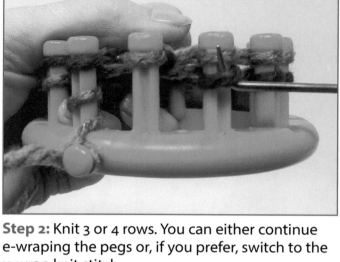

Step 4: Take the two yarn ends and knot them together. Cut off the tails down to the knot. Apply super glue to the knot.

I-Cord Toys

Simple and fast to create, I-Cord can be used as toys or to hang other toys. Spruce them up by using multiple strands or decorating with tiny pom-poms.

Skill Level:
Beginner

Skills Learned:
2-Peg I-Cord (p. 41), 3-Peg I-Cord (p. 42)

Time to Make:
5 minutes

Finished Size:
Varies

Suggested Embellishments:
Beads (p. 96), Bells (p. 96), Fringe (p. 97), Fuzzy Yarn (p. 99), Multiple Strands (p. 99), Pom-poms (p. 97)

Pattern Notes:
Starting the 2-Peg I-Cord on Peg 12 isn't required, but a good habit to get into because it is required when you transition the I-Cord to the Drawstring Cast On for more advanced toys (p. 56).

2-Peg I-Cord

The 2-Peg I-Cord creates a thin strand that makes great kitten toys. It is also used in the **Bendy I-Cord** (p. 44), the **Snark** (p. 61) and the **Large Door Hanger** (p. 70). It is also an option for the **1-Tailed Ball** (p. 55), **2-Tailed Ball** (p. 58) and **Mouse** (p. 82).

Step 1: Tie a slip knot onto Peg 12.

Step 2: Wrap the working yarn counterclockwise around Peg 1 twice. This is a double e-wrap. Knit the bottom loop over the top.

Step 3: Wrap the working yarn clockwise around the back Peg of 12 and counterclockwise around Peg 1 to make a figure eight. Knit both pegs.

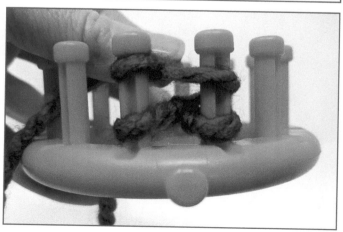

Step 4: Repeat Step 3 until the cord is the desired length. If you are creating the cord as part of a toy such as the 1-Tailed Ball or Large Door Hanger, stop after this step. If not, continue to bind off the I-cord.

Step 5: Gently pull on the loop on Peg 1 to make it larger. Then move it over to Peg 12. Once it is moved, pull on the working yarn to tighten the loop and knit.

Step 6: Cut the working yarn leaving a 2-inch tail. Loop the tail through the loop on Peg 12.

Step 7: Lift the loop off the peg and pull the tail tight. Secure it by tying a basic knot.

3-Peg I-Cord

The 3-Peg I-Cord creates a sturdy cord that cats love to toss and chase. The cord is too thick, though, to be used as hanging cords or as tails on balls.

Step 1: Tie a slip knot onto Peg 1.

Step 2: E-Wrap Peg 2 counterclockwise twice. Knit. Pull the working yarn slightly to tighten.

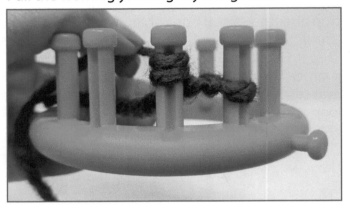

Step 3: E-Wrap Peg 3 counterclockwise twice. Knit. Pull the working yarn slightly to tighten.

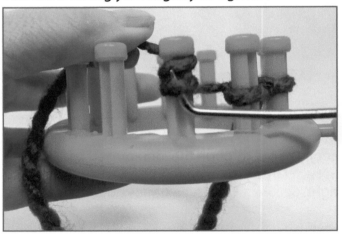

Step 4: Take working yarn behind Pegs 2 and 1, then loop it clockwise around Peg 1.

Step 5: Then loop counterclockwise around Pegs 2 & 3.

Step 6: Knit all three pegs.

Step 7: Repeat Steps 4 – 6 until the cord is as long as desired. Gently pull on the tail every few rows to set the stitches.

Step 8: Move the loop on Peg 1 over to Peg 2. Knit.

Step 9: Move the loop on Peg 3 to Peg 2. Knit.

Step 10: Trim the working yarn to leave a 2-inch tail.

Step 11: Pull the tail through the remaining loop and remove the loop from the peg.

Step 12: Lift the loop off the peg and pull the knot tight. Secure it by tying a basic knot.

Flat Knit Version

A tighter, neater version of this I-cord can be created by flat knitting the stitches instead of e-wrapping them. It is more difficult to do because you risk the stitches slipping off the peg.

After casting on (Steps 1 – 3), stretch the working yarn behind the pegs and then run it across the front of all three pegs above the existing loops. Essentially, you are wrapping all three pegs clockwise. Knit Peg 2 first. Then, knit Pegs 1 and 3. When ready to finish, follow Steps 8 – 12.

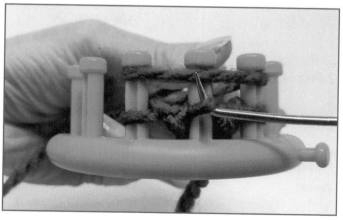

Bendy I-Cord

My cat Minx has a toy stuffed snake that she loves. Like any favorite toy, it's wearing out and I've been unable to find a replacement. The Bendy I-Cord was one of my many attempts to create a toy she might like better. In true cat fashion, Minx has chosen not to take the bait. But other cats seem to like this toy.

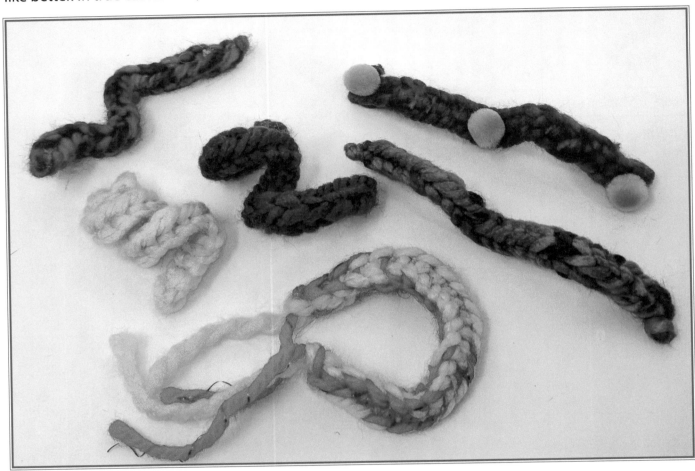

Skill Level:
Developing

Skills Required:
2-Peg I-Cord (p. 41)

Time to Make:
5 minutes

Finished Size:
Varies

Materials Required:
Pipe Cleaner

Suggested Embellishments:
Fringe (p. 97), Multiple Strands (p. 99), Pom-poms (p. 97)

Pattern Notes:
The Bendy I-Cord is easier to make if you start with a short pipe cleaner, about 3 inches long. Later, you can create longer ones if desired. Don't worry too much if the tip of the pipe cleaner is sticking out when you begin. You can adjust the yarn and secure it with glue after you are finished to cover it up. Because the ends are often sharp, either file the ends of the pipe cleaner or fold the end in to create a blunt end.

Step 1: Cut a small section of pipe cleaner to whatever length you want to make the toy.

Step 2: Start a 2-Peg I-Cord, but stop after knitting one row in Step 4.

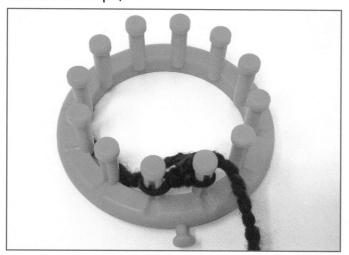

Step 3: Insert one end of the pipe cleaner into the start of the knitting between Pegs 12 and 1. Don't worry if the end pokes out. You can adjust the cord around it when you are done. The cord should rest in between the two pegs without you having to hold it.

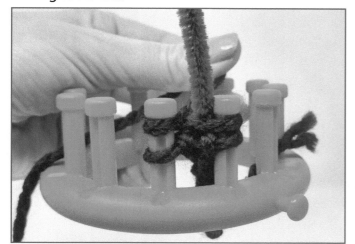

Step 4: Continue knitting by wrapping the yarn around the pipe cleaner. When you start a row, you will loop the yarn around the back of the pipe cleaner, clockwise around Peg 12, then in front of the pipe cleaner and counterclockwise around Peg 1. Knit and repeat.

Step 5: When the entire pipe cleaner has been knitted over, continue knitting 1 to 3 rows to ensure the entire pipe cleaner is covered. Bind off as normal for the I-Cord.

Step 6: When done, adjust the knitting to cover the entire pipe cleaner. Secure each end with an extra square knot, trim off the excess tail and secure with a drop of super glue.

Butterfly

I-Cords can be used to make a lot of different things. If you add a pipe cleaner, it can create a neat butterfly. Hopefully, it will encourage your cat to leave the real ones alone!

Skill Level:
Beginner

Skills Required:
2-Peg I-Cord (p. 41)

Time to Make:
20 minutes

Finished Size:
4-by-4 inches

Materials Required:
Pipe Cleaner

Suggested Embellishments:
Multiple Strands (p. 99)

Pattern Notes:
The hardest part about creating the Butterfly is getting the wings right. I recommend starting by tying yarn around it first. The yarn is easier to untie and adjust than the pipe cleaners. Once you have the wings the way you want them, you can add the pipe cleaners and the cut the yarn to remove it.

Step 1: Create a 2-Peg I-Cord that is at least 20 inches long.

Step 2: Tie the two ends together to create a loop. Trim the tails to get them out of your way.

Step 3: Lay the piece on a flat surface with the knot at the top. Stretch it out it is laid out with two halves of the cords next to each other.

Step 4: Figure out where the middle of the cords are and wrap the smaller piece of pipe cleaner (or yarn) around that spot. You are essentially creating a figure 8 with the I-Cord loop.

Step 5: Take the center of the top loop (which should be the knots) and the center of the bottom loom and bring them together.

Step 6: Take your longer Pipe Cleaner and wrap it around the top and bottom I-Cords and the middle pipe cleaner. You want to wrap it so that it leaves about 1-1/2 inches of each end at the top. The ends become the antennae of the butterfly.

Step 7: Twist the two ends together to secure.

Squirrely Q

Squirrely Q's are 2-peg curly I-Cords, also called spiral cords and curly cords. They are just the right size for your cat to carry or toss around. They are also used in the Octopus (p. 64), Small Twisty Door Hanger (p. 67) and Jellyfish (p. 87). It is optional for the 1-Tailed Ball (p. 55), 2-Tailed Ball (p. 58), Large Door Hanger (p. 70), and Mouse (p. 82).

Skill Level:
Beginner

Skills Learned:
2-Peg Curly Cord (p. 49)

Time to Make:
5 minutes

Finished Size:
Varies

Suggested Embellishments:
Beads (p. 96), Bells (p. 96), Fringe (p. 97), Fuzzy Yarn (p. 99), Multiple Strands (p. 99)

Pattern Notes:
The fun part about curly cords is that the more times you knit the repeating peg, the "curlier" the cord becomes. For solo toys, try tying the ends together or adding bells or fringe to the end. Multiple thinner strands of yarn (light or medium weight) are a quick way to add color to the toy and practice knitting using multiple cords.

Loose 2-Peg Curly I-Cord

Step 1: Tie a slip knot onto Peg 12.

Step 2: E-Wrap the working yarn around Peg 1 counterclockwise twice. Knit the bottom loop over the top loop. Tug on the working cord slightly to tighten.

Step 3: E-Wrap Peg 12 clockwise. Knit. Pull the working yarn slightly to tighten the knot.

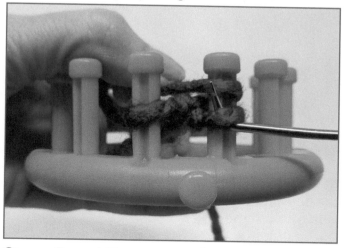

Step 4: Repeat Step 3 two or three more times. Repeating it 3 times will give you a curlier cord.

Step 5: Wrap the yarn around Peg 1 counterclockwise. Knit.

Step 6: Repeat Steps 3 – 5. Make sure to knit Peg 12 the same number of times as you did originally.

Step 7: When the cord is as long as you want, move the loop from Peg 1 to Peg 12. Knit.

Step 8: Cut the yarn leaving a 2-inch tail. Loop the tail through the loop on Peg 12, then lift the loop off the peg and pull the knot tight. Secure it by tying a basic knot.

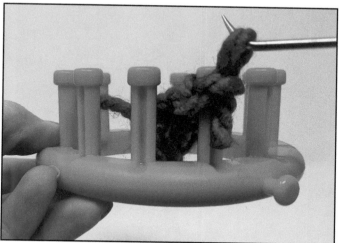

Tight 2-Peg Curly I-Cord

Step 1: Tie a slip knot onto Peg 12.

Step 2: E-Wrap Peg 2 counterclockwise twice. Knit the bottom loop over the top. Tug the working cord slightly to tighten.

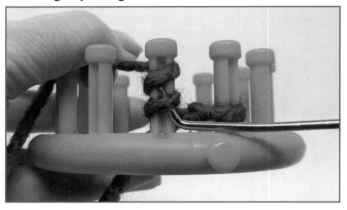

Step 3: E-Wrap the working yarn counterclockwise around Peg 1 twice. Knit the bottom loop over the top 2 loops.

Step 4: E-Wrap the yarn clockwise around Peg 12. Knit.

Step 5: Repeat Step 4 two more times.

Step 6: Wrap Peg 1 counterclockwise. Knit the bottom loop over the top 2 loops.

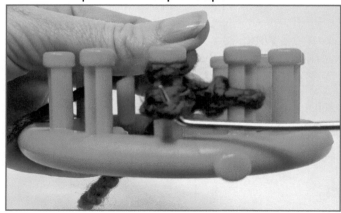

Step 7: Repeat Steps 4 – 6 until the cord is the desired length. For clarity: you knit 3 stitches on the peg with one loop and 1 stitch on the peg with on two loops.

Step 8: When ready to Bind off, knit Peg 12 once.

Step 9: Knit the bottom loop over the top on Peg 1. Each peg will only one loop at this point.

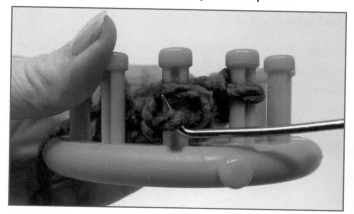

Step 10: Take the loop from Peg 1 and place it on Peg 12. Knit.

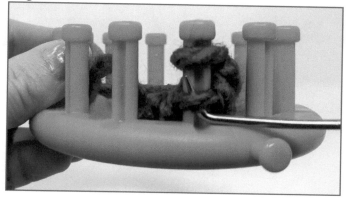

Step 11: Cut the yarn leaving a tail about 1-1/2 inches long. Loop the tail through the remaining loop and then remove it from the loom.

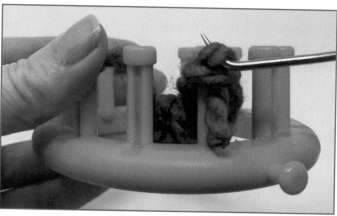

Step 12: Pull the tail to tighten. For security, tie an additional knot in the end. Trim the excess tail and secure with super glue.

Which Curly Cord to Use

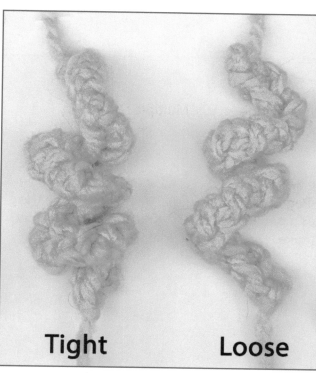

Tight   **Loose**

Two versions of the 2-Peg Curly Cord were included to give you a choice. And they are interchangeable whenever they are used because the differences between them are minor. The loose version is easier to do, in my opinion, but not by much. In contract, the tight version has a neater appearance, again in my opinion.

In the picture (left) you can see the difference between the two curly cords. Both were done with three stitches repeats on Peg 12. As you can see, the tight version creates a tighter curl with few repeats. To get the same amount of curl with the loose version, you would need to repeat Peg 12 four times.

And that's one of the great things about the curly cord: you can adjust how curly they are by how many times you repeat Peg 12. You want a cord with less curl? Knit Peg 12 twice. Need a curlier cord? Knit Peg 12 four times. It's fun to experiment with the differences until you find one you like.

 Q-Ball

The Q-Ball is a fancy name for the 3-Peg Curly Cord. It's a great toy by itself and an option for the **Large Door Hanger** (p. 70).

Skill Level:
Beginner

Skills Learned:
3-Peg Curly Cord

Time to Make:
10 minutes

Finished Size:
Varies

Suggested Embellishments:
Beads (p. 96), Bells (p. 96), Fringe (p. 97), Multiple Strands (p. 99)

Pattern Notes:
Learning to create the 3-Peg Curly Cord is easy especially if you've mastered the **Tight 2-Peg Curly Cord** (p. 50). The 3-Peg is done the same way except it has a peg in the middle. Knitting the Q-Ball with multiple strands will make it tighter and curlier.

3-Peg Curly I-Cord

Step 1: Tie a slip knot onto Peg 1.

Step 2: E-Wrap Peg 2 counterclockwise twice. Knit the bottom loop over the top. Tug the working cord slightly to tighten.

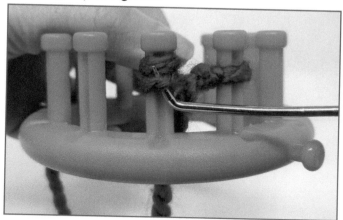

Step 3: Repeat Step 2 on Peg 3.

Step 4: Wrap the working cord around Peg 3 counterclockwise two times so there are three loops on Peg 3. Knit the bottom loop over the top 2 loops. There will always be 2 loops on Peg 3.

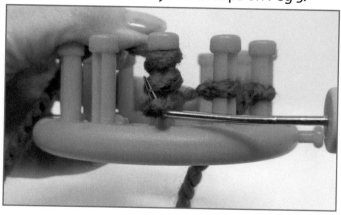

Step 5: Wrap Peg 2 and Peg 1 clockwise. Knit.

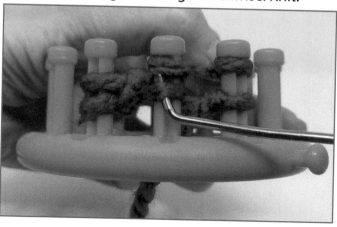

Step 6: Wrap Peg 1 clockwise, knit. (Yes, again.)

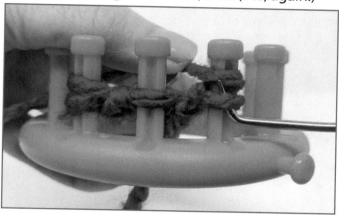

Step 7: Wrap Peg 2 counterclockwise and knit.

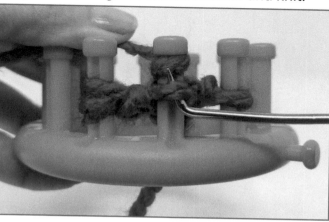

Step 8: Wrap Peg 3 counterclockwise and knit the bottom loop only.

Step 9: Repeat Steps 5 – 8 until the cord is the desired length. Note: you skip Peg 3, knit Peg 2 then knit Peg 1 twice before knitting Pegs 2 & 3.
Step 10: Move the loop on Peg 2 to Peg 1. Knit. Move the loop on Peg 1 back to Peg 2.

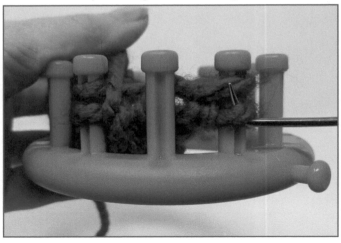

Step 11: Wrap working cord counterclockwise around Peg 3. Knit the bottom loop over the top two loops.

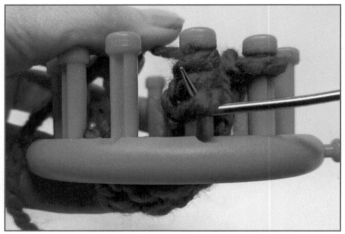

Step 12: Knit the bottom loop on Peg 3 over the top so only one loop remains.

Step 13: Knit Peg 2.
Step 14: Move the loop from Peg 2 over to Peg 3. Knit.

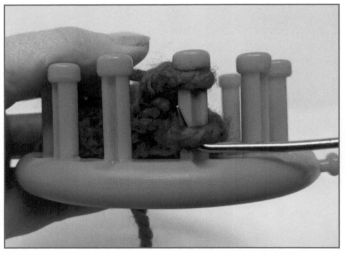

Step 15: Trim the working yarn so it is about 1-1/2 inches long. Then, pull it through the loop on the peg before removing it from the loom. Pull the tail to tighten it. Add a second knot to the end if desired. Trim excess cord and secure with glue.

One-Tailed Ball

The One-Tailed Ball started out as a failed attempt to create a mouse toy. And this pattern is a lot easier to create than the Mouse (p. 82), which starts out the same way but has a more complicated finish.

Skill Level:
Practiced

Skills Learned:
2-Peg Cord to Drawstring Cast On (p. 56)

Skills Required:
Drawstring Cast On (p. 24), Gathered Removal Bind Off (p. 25), 2-Peg I-Cord (p. 41) or 2-Peg Curly I-Cords (p. 49), Any Knit Stitch (p. 13)

Time to Make:
20 minutes

Finished Size:
4-by-2 inches (length may vary)

Materials Required:
Stuffing (p. 26)

Suggested Embellishments:
Bells (p. 96), Catnip (p. 98), Fuzzy Yarn (p. 99), Multiple Strands (p. 99), Switching Colors (p. 100)

Pattern Notes:
When you learned how to create 2-Peg Cords, it was suggested you always start them on Peg 12. That becomes essential when you create learn how to transition from the cord to the Drawstring Cast On. Learning this skill will also be used for the 2-Tailed Ball (p. 58), the Mouse (p. 82), and the Large Door Hanger (p. 73).

2-Peg Cord to Drawstring Cast On

Besides the 1-Tailed Ball, this skill is used for the **2-Tailed Ball** (p. 58), **Large Door Hanger** (p. 70), and the **Mouse** (p. 82).

Step 1: Create a 2-Peg Cord on your loom using Pegs 12 and 1. You can use either the 2-Peg I-Cord (p. 41) or one of the 2-Peg Curly Cords (p. 49). When your cord is the desired length, stop knitting after knitting Peg 12 (before knitting Peg 1).

Step 2: If Peg 1 has two loops, reduce it to one loop by knitting the bottom loop over the top.

Step 3: To start the Drawstring Cast On, you are going to take the working yarn from behind Peg 1 and in front of Peg 2 (p. 24). This is the same way you begin in the normal Drawstring Cast On when a slip knot is on the anchor peg .

Step 4: When you have weaved all the way around the loom, you are ready to start looping over. Again, do this just like you would on a regular Drawstring Cast On, except when you get to Peg 12, knit both loops over.

Step 5: Instead of skipping Peg 1 as you normally would, knit it using the loop on Peg 1.

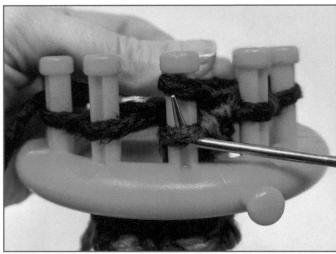

Step 6: Continue knitting as you would for a Basic Ball (p. 22).

Finishing the Ball

Step 7: Bind off with the Gathered Removal Bind Off (p. 25).

Step 8: When finished, turn the ball inside out and close the end with the Gathered Removal Bind Off. Knot it like usual.

Step 9: Stuff the ball. See Stuffing (p. 26).

Closing a Drawstring Cast On with a Tail

Step 10: Because there is no yarn tail (just an cord tail) you can't close things as you would typically by pulling on the tail. Instead, you need to locate the yarn in the knitting that will close it. When you look at that end, you will see a strand of yarn going through the loops. Grab this yarn. You will know if you found it because when you pull on it, the hole starts to close.

Step 11: Pull on this yarn so the excess yarn ends up across from the tail. When the hole has closed most of the way, cut the yarn in half so you have two ends. This will make it easier to tighten the hole and tie a knot.

Step 12: Tie the two ends into a knot and tuck them into the ball. If necessary, loop the ends onto a needle. Poke the needle through the hole at the top and through the side of the ball. You can then remove the needle and trim off the end.

Two-Tailed Ball

If your cat likes the One-Tailed Ball, it will love the two-tailed version. But why stop at just adding one tail? The Snark adds six cords (p. 61) and the Octopus adds eight (p. 64).

Skill Level:
Practiced

Skills Learned:
Integrating a Cord (p. 60)

Skills Required:
Drawstring Cast On (p. 24), Gathered Removal Bind Off (p. 25), 2-Peg I-Cord (p. 41) or 2-Peg Curly I-Cords (p. 49), 2-Peg Cord to Drawstring Cast On (p. 56), Any Knit Stitch (p. 13)

Time to Make:
30 minutes

Finished Size:
2 inches wide, 6 to 8 inches long

Materials Required:
Stuffing (p. 26)

Suggested Embellishments:
Bells (p. 96), Catnip (p. 98), Multiple Strands (p. 99), Switching Colors (p. 100)

Pattern Notes:
Adding a second tail to a ball is done by integrating the cord into the knitting. Usually, I create one cord before I start the ball. But if you have 2 skeins of yarn, you can create the cord on the loom when it is time to add it.

Create the Second Tail

Step 1: Create a 2-Peg Cord about 3 inches long. You may use either the 2-Peg I-Cord (p. 41) or the 2-Peg Curly Cord (p. 49).
Step 2: If any pegs have 2 loops, knit the bottom loop over so it only has 1 loop.
Step 3: Remove the tail from the loom. To prevent it from unraveling, place the loops onto a pen or similar round object until you are ready to use it.

Create the One-Tailed Ball

Step 4: Follow the instructions for the 1-Tailed Ball (p. 55). Stop before you bind off (Step 7).
Step 5: Decide where you want the second tail. Good options are either Pegs 6 and 7 or Pegs 12 and 1. In the image, the tail is placed on Pegs 6 and 7. Place the loops of the tail onto those pegs above the existing loops.

Multiple Tails on One End

If you want to create a ball with two tails (or more) on one end, you do so by integrating them before finishing the ball. Technically, a cord could be integrated at any point in your knitting. But if you knit more than a couple of rows after integrating, you will have to move the tail, so it is under your loom. You can learn more about integrating multiple cords when making the Snark (p. 61), the Octopus (p. 64), and the Spider (p. 76).

Integrating a Cord

Step 6: To integrate the cord, knit a row normally until you get to the pegs where the cord is placed. On these pegs, take the bottom two loops and knit them over the new loop.

Step 7: Continue until you are back at Peg 1.

Step 8: Secure the tail by pulling the tail to tighten the loops and then tying a knot. Because it will be on the inside of the ball, you don't need to trim the excess unless you want to. If you do trim, secure the knot with super glue. You can wait to do this step until after the bind off. You can also do this immediately after loops of the cord has been knitted on.

Finishing the Ball

Step 9: Finish with the Gathered Removal Bind Off (p. 25).

Step 10: Close the end with the first tail by following the instructions under "Closing a Drawstring Cast On with a Tail" (p. 57).

Step 11: Stuff the ball. See **Stuffing Toys** (p. 26).

Step 12: Close the other end. Because the tail was integrated before the Drawstring Cast On began, you don't need to do anything different to close this end.

Six-Legged Snark

Lewis Carrol first used the word "Snark" to describe a mysterious creature in his poem "The Hunting of the Snark." As he described it, "the Snark's a peculiar creature, that won't / Be caught in a commonplace way." Thankfully, this Snark isn't as challenging to catch.

Skill Level:
Proficient

Skills Required:
Drawstring Cast On (p. 24), Gathered Removal Bind Off (p. 25), 2-Peg I-Cord (p. 41), Integrating a Cord (p. 60), Any Knit Stitch (p. 13)

Time to Make:
60 minutes

Finished Size:
6-by-3 inches

Materials Required:
2nd Skein of Yarn or Extra Loom, Stuffing (p. 26)

Suggested Embellishments:
Catnip (p. 98), Felt (p. 96), Pom-poms (p. 97), Switching Colors (p. 100),

Pattern Notes:
To create the Snark, you may find it easier to make the legs on an empty loom and then move the legs to the main loom when you're ready. If you don't have a second loom, you can create the legs on your main loom when you are ready to incorporate, but you'll need a 2nd skein of yarn.

Step 1: Cast on with the Drawstring Cast On (p. 24). This is the start of the Snark's body.

Step 2: Knitting in the round until the body is about 2 inches long. You can use any knit stitch desired.

Step 3: Push the loops down to the base of the loom. You will ignore them until after you have created the legs. Set aside the yarn you are using for the body.

Step 4: On Pegs 1 and 2, create a 2-Peg I-Cord (p. 41). Once it is as long as you desire (about 2.5 inches), cut the working yarn leaving a 3-inch tail. If possible, try knitting around the beginning tail so it is tucked into the leg. Otherwise, trim off the beginning tail and secure the knot with super glue.

Step 5: Secure the leg by knitting a new stitch on these pegs. To do this, wrap your body working yarn (that you set aside in Step 3) around Peg 1 and knit the bottom two loops (the original loop and the first "leg" loop) over.

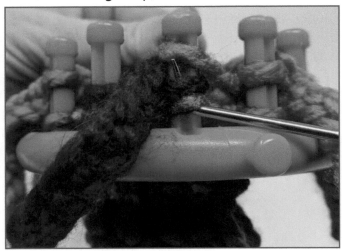

Step 6: Repeat Step 5 on Peg 2.

Step 7: Repeat Steps 4 – 6 on the remaining pegs until they all have their own leg.

Step 8: To get the legs into the right position, lift the loops up to the top of the peg. Then, pull the leg from the inside of the loom so the leg is underneath the base.

Step 9: Knit four more rows before binding off using the Gathered Removal Bind Off (p. 25).

Step 10: Turn the toy inside out so you can secure the legs. On each leg, gently tug the tail to tighten the loops. Then tie a knot.

Step 11: To further secure the legs, tie two tails together. Secure the knot with super glue, if desired. Reverse the toy so it is right side out.

Step 12: Close one end of the Snark the same way you would a basic ball (p. 22), except instead of turning the Snark inside out, close it by pulling on the tail.

Step 16: Stuff. See **Stuffing** Toys (p. 26).
Step 17: Close the other end of the Snark.

Octopus

A great buddy willing to cuddle with your kitty no matter how many times it gets attacked.

Skill Level:
Proficient

Skills Required:
Drawstring Cast On (p. 24), Gathered Removal Bind Off (p. 25), 2-Peg Curly I-Cords (p. 49), Integrating a Cord (p. 60), Any Knit Stitch (p. 13)

Time to Make:
60 minutes

Finished Size:
5-by-5-by-3.5 inches

Materials Required:
Extra Loom, Stuffing (p. 26)

Suggested Embellishments:
Catnip (p. 98), Felt (p. 96), Pom-poms (p. 97), Switching Colors (p. 100)

Pattern Notes:
The Octopus is easier to do if you have a second loom. The other loom doesn't need to be a 12-peg loom or even the same gauge since you will reduce the 2-Peg Curly Cords down to one loop before integrating. If you don't have another loom, slip them onto a pen or pencil to hold until you are ready to use.

Step 1: Create a 2-Peg Curly Cord about 2-1/2 inches long to make one leg (p. 49).

Step 2: When the leg is about 2 inches long, take the last loop added and move it over the other peg. Knit the bottom loop over the top.

Step 3: Leave the leg on the peg. Trim the working yarn to leave a 2- to 3-inch tail.

Step 4: Repeat Steps 1 – 3 to create 7 additional legs. If you only have one loom, you can move the legs onto a pen or similar object to free your loom to create the body.

Step 5: On an empty loom, cast on using the Drawstring Cast On (p. 24).

Step 6: Knit using any stitch until it is about 1-1/2 to 2 inches long. Once the body is as long as desired, you are ready to integrate your legs.

Step 7: Knit Peg 1.

Step 8: Add one leg to Peg 2.

Step 9: Knit Peg 2, but knit both the bottom loop and the leg loops over the new one.

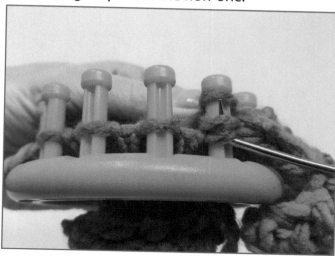

Step 10: You can now tie a knot in the tail of the leg to secure it. Trim the tail.

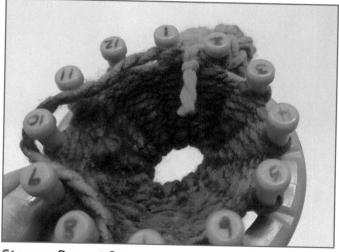

Step 11: Repeat Steps 8 – 10 to secure legs to Pegs 3, 4, and 5.

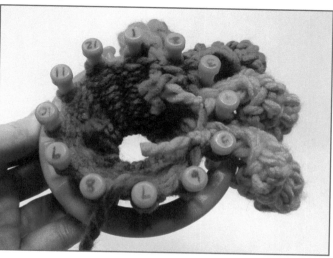

Step 12: Knit Pegs 6 and 7.

Step 13: Repeat Steps 8 – 10 to secure legs to Pegs 8, 9, 10, and 11.

Step 16: Close one end of the Octopus the same way you would a basic ball (p. 22). Except instead of turning the Octopus inside out, close it by pulling on the tail.

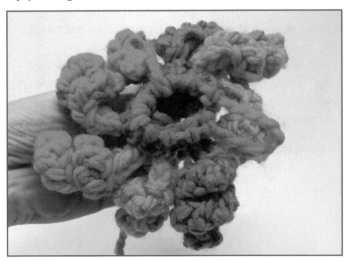

Step 14: Knit another row around the loom.

Step 15: Finish with the Gathered Removal Bind Off (p. 25).

Step 17: Stuff. See **Stuffing Toys** (p. 26).

Step 18: Close the other end of the Octopus.

Small Twisty Door Hanger

This smaller version of the door hanger is fun for cats to swat. You can create a shorter version to tie in your cat's crate to make travel a little easier.

Skill Level:
Developing

Skills Learned:
1-Peg I-Cord (p. 69)

Skills Required:
2-Peg Curly I-Cords (p. 49)

Time to Make:
20 minutes

Finished Size:
14 to 16 inches long

Suggested Embellishments:
Bells (p. 96), Fringe (p. 97),
Multiple Strands (p. 99),
Switching Colors (p. 100)

Pattern Notes:
The Small Twisty Door Hanger combines the 1-Peg I-Cord with either of the 2-Peg Curly Cords. It's easier to create these if you have an idea of where you want to hang it so you can get the measurements right. Remember to hang high and supervise!

Step 1: Create a 1-Peg I-Cord 8 inches long (p. 69).

Step 2: To create a hanging loop, tie the tail loosely on to the cord using a half-knot.

Step 3: Continue knitting the I-Cord. After 1 or 2 stitches, tighten the tail and add another half knot to secure. You can then trim off the end and secure with super glue.

Step 4: Continue knitting the I-Cord until it is about 12 inches long.

Step 5: Place the last loop of the I-cord onto Peg 1.

Step 6: E-Wrap Peg 2 and knit. You are now set to do the Loose 2-Peg Curly Cord (p. 49). If you want to do the Tight Curly Cord, go onto Step 7. Otherwise, go to Step 8.

Step 7 (optional): E-Wrap Peg 2 twice and knit the bottom loop over the top 2 loops. You are now set to do a Tight 2-Peg Curly Cord (p. 50).

Step 8: Follow the instructions for either of the 2-Peg Curly Cords, including the bind off.

1-Peg I-Cord

Trying to do a 1-Peg I-Cord on a loom is tricky because without a second peg, nothing prevents the knitting from spinning on the peg. So I figured out a way to do it without the loom. The cord is a little sturdier than just a strand of yarn when hanging toys. It's also used with the Spider (p. 76) and Jellyfish (p. 87) plus is an option for the Mouse (p. 82).

Step 1: Make a slip knot. Pull on the loop to make it slightly larger than usual.

Step 2: While holding the knot in one hand, reach through the loop with your other hand to grab the working yarn and pull it through the loop to create a new loop.

Step 3: Grasp the new loop in one hand and the slip knot in your other and gently pull until the new knot is tight against the slip knot. Don't worry about how large the new loop gets.

Step 4: Reduce the size of the new loop by holding on the knot and pulling the working yarn.

Step 5: Repeat Steps 2 – 4 until the cord is as long as you need it.

Large Door Hanger

Although these three toys may look different, they are actually variations of the Ball Door Hanger (center toy). The Twisty Door Hanger (right) swaps the ball for a 3-Peg Curly Cord. Meanwhile, the Curly Ball Door Hanger (left) uses a 2-peg curly cord instead of an I-Cord after you create the loop for the door handle. All three are sure to provide hours of fun for your kitty.

Skill Level:
Developing

Skills Required:
2-Peg I-Cord (p. 41), 2-Peg Curly I-Cords (p. 49), 3-Peg Curly Cord (p. 53), Gathered Removal Bind Off (p. 25), 2-Peg Cord to Drawstring Cast On (p. 56), Any Knit Stitch (p. 13)

Time to Make:
25 minutes

Finished Size:
14 to 18 inches long

Materials Required:
Stuffing (p. 26)

Suggested Embellishments:
Bells (p. 96), Fringe (p. 97), Switching Colors (p. 100)

Pattern Notes:
When creating a door hanger, you want it long enough to slip over whatever you plan to hang it on, like a doorknob. For safety, have this toy hang high enough that your cat or kitten has to reach for it. Otherwise, they could get it wrapped around themselves and be in danger of choking.

2-Peg I-Cord Hanger

Step 1: Create a 2-Peg I-Cord about 7 inches long on Pegs 12 and 1 (p. 41). This piece will need to be long enough to create a loop that can slip over a doorknob.

Step 2: Locate the first two loops from the beginning end of the I-Cord. They don't have to be precisely the first two loops, as long as they are near the end.

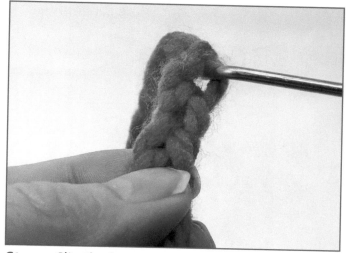

Step 3: Slip the loops onto the pegs you are using. Make sure the I-Cord isn't twisted and that your working yarn doesn't get trapped between the loops.

Step 4: Wrap the working yarn around the pegs like you would normally for a 2-Peg I-Cord. Knit the bottom two loops over the top loop. You now have a loop that can go over the doorknob.

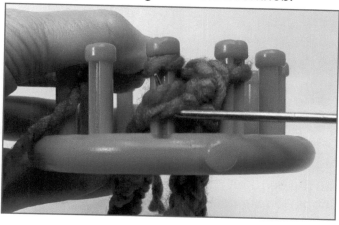

Step 5: Continue knitting the I-Cord until it is about 12 inches long or switch to a curly cord to create the Curly Ball Door Hanger (see below).

Curly Ball Door Hanger (Alternate Step 5)
If you plan on doing the Ball Door Hanger, consider using a 2-Peg Tight Curly Cord instead of the I-Cord in Step 5. To do this, wrap the yarn twice around Peg 1 (creating three loops). Knit the bottom loop over the top two. Follow the instructions for the tight curly cord (p. 50).

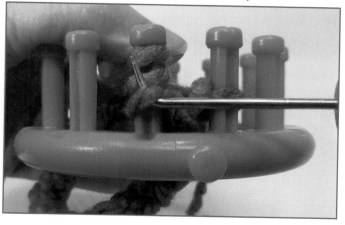

Since the ball can weigh down the curly cord, you want to do more curling loops and create a shorter cord. For the Tight Curly Cord, knit the single loop peg at least four times.

Adding a 3-Peg Curly Cord

Step 6: Cast on Peg 2 by e-wrapping it twice and knitting the bottom loop over the top loop.

Step 7: Wrap Peg 3 two times, creating three loops on the peg. Knit the bottom loop over the top two loops. You are now ready to start the 3-Peg Curly Cord (p. 53).

Step 8: When the Curly Cord is as long as desired, stop knitting on Peg 1 (before you would knit the double wrapped peg).

Step 9: Move the loop from Peg 1 over to Peg 12. Knit. Move the loop back to Peg 1.

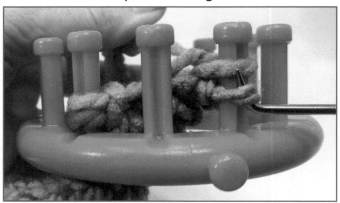

Step 10: On Peg 3, knit the bottom loop over the top leaving one loop on the peg.

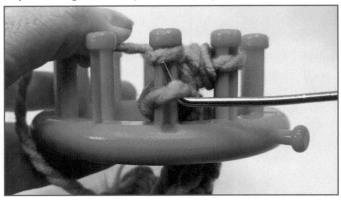

Step 11: Knit Peg 2.

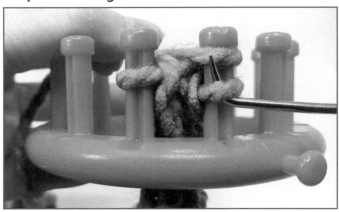

Step 12: Move the loop from Peg 2 over to Peg 3. Knit.

Step 13: Trim the working yarn so it is 1-1/2 inches long. Then, pull it through the loop on the peg before removing it from the loom. Pull the tail to tighten it. Add a knot to the end.

Adding a Ball

Although complete instructions are provided here, you can get more information about how to transition from the I-cord to the ball in the sections 2-Peg Cord to Drawstring Cast On (p. 56) and Closing a Drawstring Cast on with a Tail (p. 57).

Step 6: To start the Drawstring Cast On, you are going to take the yarn from behind Peg 1 and in front of Peg 2 (p. 24). This is just like you would in the normal Drawstring Cast On started with a slip knot on the anchor peg.

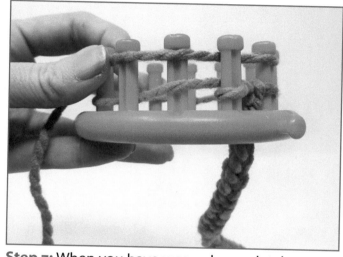

Step 7: When you have weaved completely around the loom, you are ready to start looping over. Again, do this just like you would on a regular Drawstring Cast on, except when you get to Peg 12, knit both loops over.

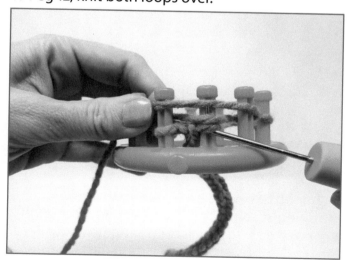

Step 8: Instead of skipping Peg 1, knit it using the loop from the tail.

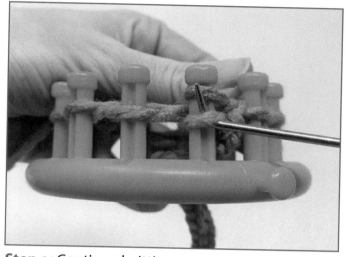

Step 9: Continue knitting as you would for a Basic Ball, including binding off with the Gathered Removal Bind Off (p. 25).

Step 10: To close the end with the tail, you will need to find the loop that will tighten it. As you look at it, you'll notice that the yarn goes through the loops. The first loop is the one you need to pull to tighten it. Grab the yarn across from the tail. When you tug it slightly, you'll notice that the hole starts to close. Pull as much as you can, then cut the yarn in two. Tie the two ends into a knot and tuck them into the ball.

Disc

I got this idea after seeing a pair of knitted earrings. These small discs are perfect for cats and kittens to swat, bounce, and chase and will keep your cat busy for days. It is also the foundation for the **Spider** (p. 76).

Skill Level:
Developing

Skills Required:
U-Wrap Knit Stitch (p. 15), E-Wrap Cast On (p. 33), Gathered Removal Bind Off (p. 25)

Time to Make:
5 minutes

Finished Size:
2-by-2 inches

Suggested Embellishments:
Fuzzy Yarn (p. 99), **Multiple Strands** (p. 99)

Pattern Notes:
Be careful to keep track of how many rows you are doing. If you do too many, you'll end up with a cupped disc. These discs can also be made in "reverse" if you use the **Drawstring Cast On** (p. 24), knit 2-3 rows and then complete with the **Basic Bind Off** (p. 36).

Step 1: Cast on using the E-Wrap Cast On (p. 33). For best results, use the Advanced Method.

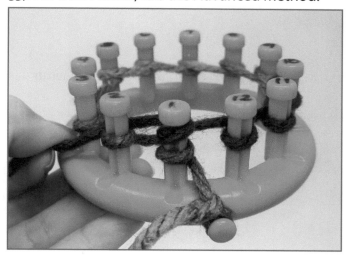

Step 2: Knit 2 to 3 rows with the u-wrap knit stitch. Two rows if using super bulky yarn. Three rows if using bulky yarn.

Step 3: Bind off using the Gathered Removal Bind Off (p. 25).

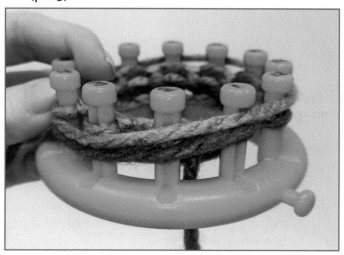

Step 4: Pull on the tail to close the end. Tie a knot to secure.

Step 5: Loop the tail for the opposite through one of the loops of the cast on and knot it.

Step 6: Cut both tails and secure the knots with super glue.

Spider

Finally, a spider that won't send you running for a can of insect spray when you see your cat playing with it! The Spider is simply the Disc with I-Cord legs.

Skill Level:
Practiced

Skills Required:
U-Wrap Knit Stitch (p. 15), E-Wrap Cast On (p. 33), Integrating a Cord (p. 60), 1-Peg I-Cord (p. 69), Gathered Removal Bind Off (p. 25)

Time to Make:
25 minutes

Finished Size:
2-by-5 inches

Suggested Embellishments:
Pom-poms (p. 97)

Pattern Notes:
The hardest part of creating this toy is keeping all the legs straight without tangling the yarn, which is why I recommend securing each leg as soon as you've knitted it on. Be sure to add a drop of super glue or the legs may detatch.

Step 1: Create eight 1-Peg I-Cords about 3 inches long (p. 69). Leave enough of a tail on each leg so you can tie a knot.

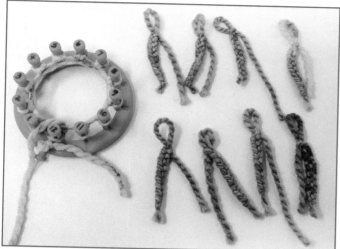

Step 2: Cast on with the E-Wrap Cast On (p. 33).

Step 3: Knit Peg 1 with using the u-wrap knit stitch.

Step 4: Add one of the legs to Peg 2. Place the leg so the tail of the leg is on the right side. Turn the leg slightly to present the loop which will make it easier to knit both loops over the working yarn loop.

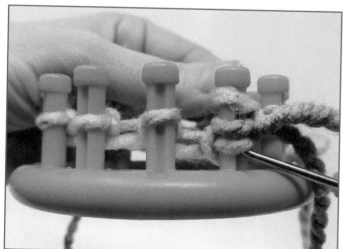

Step 5: Secure the leg by pulling the tail and tying a knot. Trim the end close to the knot and secure it with a drop of super glue.

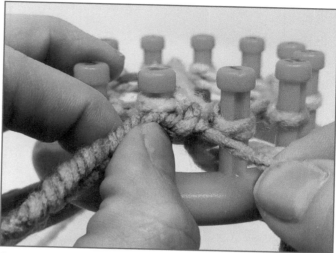

Step 6: Repeat Steps 4 & 5 on Pegs 3, 4, and 5. Knit Pegs 6 and 7 normally. Then, repeat Steps 3 & 4 on Pegs 8, 9, 10, and 11. Knit Peg 12 normally.

Step 7: Knit two more rows.

Step 8: Bind off using the Gathered Removal Bind Off (p. 25).

Step 9: Pull closed by gently on the tail. Tie a knot and secure with super glue.

Step 10: Tie a knot to secure the yarn on the other end. Cut the yarn close to the knot and secure with super glue.

Step 11: Use small pom-poms for eyes if desired.

Flower & Hoop

The Flower and Hoop are toys small enough for your cat to carry and light enough to bat across the floor. This is a trickier toy to make until you get the hang of it, so be warned.

Skill Level:
Proficient

Skills Required:
E-Wrap Knit Stitch (p. 14), U-Wrap Knit Stitch (p. 15), E-Wrap Cast On (p. 33), Gathered Removal Bind Off (p. 25) or Basic Bind Off (p. 36)

Time to Make:
20 minutes

Finished Size:
2.5-by-1.5 inches

Materials Needed:
Large pom-pom or bell (flower finish)

Suggested Embellishments:
Multiple Strands (p. 99),

Pattern Notes:
Two ways to finish this toy gives you a lot of variety. Also, if you do the flower finish, you will be knitting a tiny stocking hat. So when you master the skill, try it out on a larger loom for a hat you can wear.

Step 1: Cast on with the E-Wrap Cast On (p. 33).

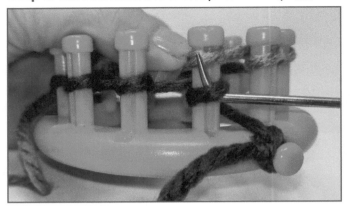

Step 2: Knit about 7 rows using the e-wrap knit stitch. Make sure your working yarn remains between Pegs 12 and 1 and lies to the outside of the loom before you start the next step.

Step 3: Grab the beginning edge of your knitting and fold it up to the pegs. Find one of the loops at the start of the piece and place it back onto the loom. Continue to do this until all the loops are on the loom. If you start out right, the loops should line up with the pegs.

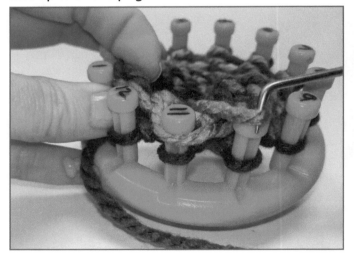

Step 4: Continue adding the loops to the loom. Tuck the starting tail into the middle.

Step 5: Knit the bottom loop over the top one for all 12 pegs.

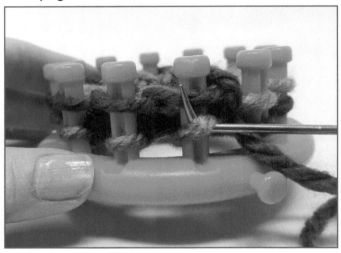

There are two different ways to finish this toy. See the next page for each version.

Flower

Ring

Flower Finish

Step 6: Continue knitting using the u-wrap knit stitch for 5 rows.

Step 7: Bind off using the Gathered Removal Bind Off (p. 25).

Step 8: Invert the knitting and close the top by pulling on the tail. Knot the end and trim.

Step 9: Invert the knitting back.
Step 10: Glue a large pom-pom into the middle. Alternatively, you can also tie a large bell into the middle.

Ring Finish

Step 6: Bind off with the Basic Bind Off (p. 36).

Step 7: Loop the tail through one of the loops near the beginning of the bind off and tie a knot.

Step 8: Trim the end and secure the knot with super glue.

Mouse

There is a relatively unknown law that requires any book about cat toys to include some type of mouse. Okay, it may not be a law, but it does feel like a requirement for a book to be complete.

Skill Level:
Proficient

Skills Required:
2-Peg Curly I-Cords (p. 49) or 2-Peg I-Cord (p. 41), 2-Peg Cord to Drawstring Cast On (p. 56), Drawstring Cast On (p. 24), Any Knit Stitch (p. 13)

Time to Make:
35 minutes

Finished Size:
4-by-2 inches (not including tail)

Materials Required:
Stuffing (p. 26), Embroidery Needle, Super glue

Suggested Embellishments:
Bells (p. 96), Catnip (p. 98), Fuzzy Yarn (p. 99), **Multiple Strands** (p. 99), **Switching Colors** (p. 100)

Pattern Notes:
The ears and whiskers are optional. Make sure they are completely secure before closing up the mouse. If you decide to create a mouse using fuzzy yarn, integrate the yarn after you've made the tail and done the Drawstring Cast On. It makes it easier to pull the drawstring close.

Creating the Body

Step 1: Create either a 2-Peg I-Cord (p. 41) or 2-Peg Curly Cord (p. 49) onto Pegs 12 and 1.

Step 2: Follow the instructions for the 2-Peg Cord to Drawstring Cast On, creating a cord about 3 to 4 inches long (p. 56).

Step 3: Knit several rows of u-wrap stitches until you get about an inch of stitches.

Step 4: Knit Pegs 1 through 6 and stop. You are now going to switch knitting directions and reduce things by one peg. Wrap the yarn around Peg 5 (instead of 7) and knit.

Step 5: Enlarge the newly-made loop on Peg 5 to make it larger. Move it over to Peg 6. Pull on the working yarn to tighten the loop and then knit.

Step 6: Move the loop from Peg 6 back to Peg 5. You an pull it slightly to make it larger if necessary. Once it is on Peg 5, pull on the working yarn to tighten. Peg 6 is now empty.

Step 7: You are now going to knit in the reverse direction (counterclockwise) for one row.

Step 8: When you reach Peg 7, you will reverse directions again and reduce. This time, knit Peg 8, move the loop to Peg 7. Knit and then return the loop to Peg 8. Pull on the working yarn to tighten as needed.

Step 9: Repeat Steps 5 – 8 until only 3 pegs remain. To summarize the steps: Switch direction when you hit the end or the row. Knit the 2nd to last peg. Move it to the last peg and knit. Then move this loop back to the 2nd to last peg (which is now the last peg). When you are done, you should only have loops on Pegs 1, 12 and 11.

Step 10: Knit Pegs 12 and 11.

Step 11: Reverse direction and knit Peg 12.

Step 12: Move the loop on Peg 12 to Peg 11 and knit.

Step 13: Instead of moving the loop back to Peg 12, move it so it is above Peg 1. Knit. You now have only one loop left.

Step 14: Cut the working yarn to leave about a 5-inch tail. You will later use this tail to sew the mouse closed.

Step 15: Loop the yarn tail through the last loop and remove the loop from the loom.

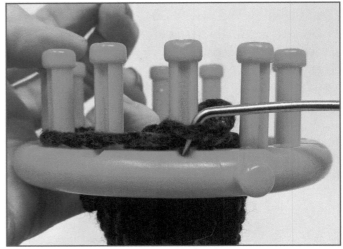

Step 16: Pull on the yarn tail to tighten.

Adding Ears

Step 1: Take a piece of yarn about 8 inches long and thread it onto a needle.

Step 2: Starting from the underside of the body, sew two loops to create ears. Make sure the ears are placed where you want before continuing.

Step 3: To secure the ears, use a bit of super glue to secure the knot to the loop on the inside (between the two ears).

Adding Whiskers

Step 1: Cut three pieces of thin yarn about 7 inches long. Tie multiple knots in the center of the strands.

Step 2: Thread one side of the whiskers onto a needle and pull it threw the backside of the fabric.

Step 3: Repeat Step 3 with the other side of the whiskers.

Step 4: To prevent the whiskers from being tugged through the fabric, secure the knot to the fabric with super glue.

Closing the Mouse

Step 1: Thread the tail at the end of the nose onto a needle.

Step 2: If you look at the sides of the mouse you will notice rows of Vs on each side. To sew close, you sew back and forth through the Vs.

Step 3: Tie a knot in the end of the tail. The knot should be on the inside of the mouse. It is easier you turn the mouse slightly inside out to get the knot tight.

Step 4: Stuff the mouse as desired (p. 26).

Step 5: Close the other as explained in "Closing a Drawstring Cast on with a Tail" (p. 57).

How to go from a 1-Peg I-Cord to a Drawstring Cast On.

Knit a 1-Peg I-Cord as long as you want it to create the tail (p. 69). Place the loop you knitted last onto Peg 12 . Then, take the working yarn between Pegs 1 and 2 and weave it like normal for the **Drawstring Cast On** (p. 24).

Jellyfish

The Jellyfish started as a failed attempt to knit a rose from a YouTube video. But from that failure came my favorite toy in the book.

Skill Level:
Proficient

Skills Required:
Gathered Removal Bind Off (p. 25), 2-Peg Curly I-Cords (p. 49), Integrating a Cord (p. 60), 1-Peg I-Cord (p. 69), U-Wrap Knit Stitch (p. 15)

Time to Make:
75 minutes

Finished Size:
3-by-6-inches (not including hanging cord)

Materials Needed:
2 Bells

Preparation

Step 1: Create a bell tentacle by creating a 4-1/2 inch long 1-Peg I-Cord (p. 69). Attach a bell to the beginning end. Trim the working yarn so it leaves a tail at least as long as the I-Cord.

Step 2: Create a 2-Peg Curly Cord about 2-1/2 inches long (p. 49). Knit the right peg last.

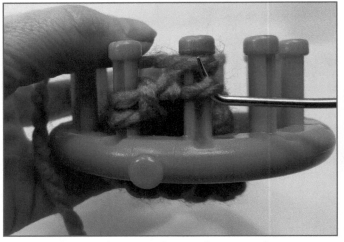

Step 3: If a peg has two loops, knit one loop over.

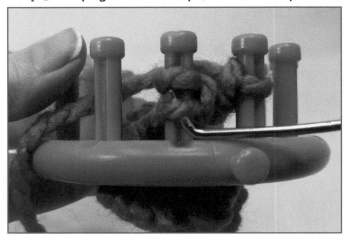

Step 4: Move the right peg over above the other peg. Knit.

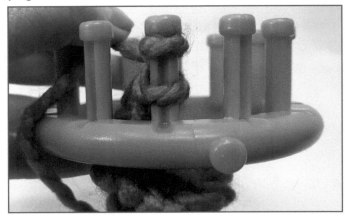

Step 5: Wrap your cord around the peg and knit. Repeat. Tug on the loop that's on the peg to make it larger. Remove it from the loom. Transition to the 1-Peg I-Cord. Make this tentacle the same length as the one with the bell. Trim the working cord so it is at least as long as the tentacle.

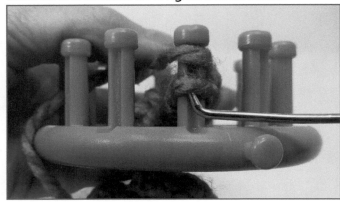

Step 6: Repeat Steps 1 – 6 to create two additional tentacles.

First Side

Step 1: Secure your slip knot onto Peg 1.

Step 2: E-Wrap the yarn counterclockwise around the middle of Pegs 2 and 3. Then u-wrap around Peg 4 by going around behind and to the front it.

Step 3: E-Wrap Pegs 3, 2, & 1 clockwise.

Step 4: Knit pegs 3, 2, & 1.

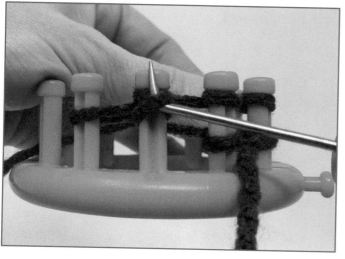

Step 5: Skip Peg 1. U-Wrap and knit Pegs 2, 3, & 4.

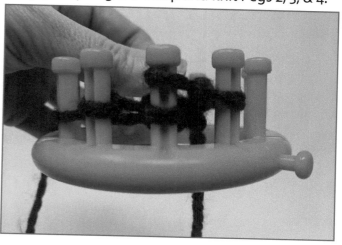

Step 6: Skip Peg 4. U-Wrap and knit Peg 3, 2, & 1.

Step 7: Repeat Steps 5 & 6 twice.

Step 8: Skip Peg 1. U-Wrap and knit Pegs 2, 3, and 4. (This is a repeat of Step 5.)

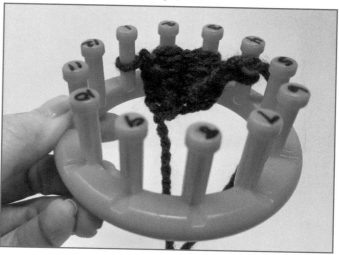

The next three sections are a repeat of the first part. The last peg knitted on each side serves as the first peg of the next sides. The steps are listed to help you keep track of which pegs you are using. Don't worry if you lose count of how many rows you've done. Compare the new side with an existing one. If they look the same length, you're fine.

Second Side

Step 9: E-Wrap the yarn around the middle of Pegs 5 and 6. Then u-wrap around Peg 7 by going around behind and to the front it.
Step 10: E-Wrap Pegs 6, 5 & 4. Knit all three pegs
Step 11: Skip Peg 4. U-Wrap and knit Pegs 5, 6 & 7.

Step 12: Skip Peg 7. U-Wrap knit Peg 6, 5 & 4.
Step 13: Repeat Steps 10 and 11 twice.
Step 14: Skip Peg 4. U-Wrap knit Pegs 5, 6 & 7. (This is a repeat of Step 11.)

Third Side

Step 15: E-Wrap the yarn around the middle of Pegs 8 and 9. Then u-wrap around Peg 10 by going around behind and to the front it.
Step 16: E-Wrap Pegs 9, 8 & 7 and then knit.
Step 17: Skip Peg 7. U-Wrap and knit Pegs 8, 9 & 10.

Step 18: Skip Peg 10. U-Wrap knit Peg 9, 8 and 7.
Step 19: Repeat Steps 16 and 17 twice.
Step 20: Skip Peg 7. U-Wrap knit Pegs 8, 9 and 10. (This is a repeat of Step 17.)

Fourth Side

Step 21: E-Wrap the yarn around the middle of Pegs 11 and 12. Then u-wrap around Peg 1 by going around behind and to the front it.
Step 22: E-Wrap Pegs 12, 11 & 10 and then knit. Ignore the loop already on Peg 1 for now.

Step 23: Skip Peg 10. U-Wrap and knit Pegs 11, 12 & 1. Again, ignore the original loop on Peg 1.
Step 24: Skip Peg 1. U-Wrap knit Peg 12, 11 & 10.
Step 25: Repeat Steps 22 and 23 twice.
Step 26: Skip Peg 10. U-Wrap knit Pegs 11, 12 & 1. (This is a repeat of Step 23.)

Now that you have this part done, you are ready to integrate the pieces created in the first part and bind off the Jellyfish.

Center Piece

Step 27: Knit the bottom loop on Peg 1 over the top one to connect the ends.

Step 28: Add the four extra pieces onto Pegs 3, 6, 9, and 12. The pieces should be placed so they hangs to the inside of the loom.

Step 29: Knit Pegs 2 – 12 using the u-wrap knit stitch. When you get to a peg with an extra piece, knit both loops over the new one.

Step 30: Knit three more rows using the u-wrap knit stitch.

Step 31: Bind off using the Gathered Removal Bind Off (p. 25). When you cut the working yarn for this step, don't cut it too short. Keep it about 4 inches long.

Finishing

Step 32: Close the Gathered Removal Bind Off like normal, but don't trim the tail (p. 25).

Step 34: Tie a knot at the end of each tail to prevent it from unraveling. Trim the excess yarn and secure the knot with glue.

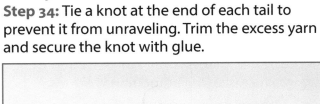

Step 33: Secure the four tentacles by pulling on the tail and tying a knot. Do not trim the tail. Instead, you are going to let it hang to add extra interest to the toy.

Step 35: Tie an extra knot in the beginning tail of the body and trim the excess yarn. Secure the knot with super glue.

Hanging Cord

This toy works best by hanging. And while you can tie it using the tail left over from the Gathered Removal Bind Off (especially if you cut it longer than normal) it looks better if you add a cord by creating a 1-Peg I-Cord.

Step 36: Create a 1-Peg I-Cord about 15 inches long, or however long you want (p. 69). The starting tail needs to be at least 2 to 3 inches long so you can secure it to the Jellyfish.

Step 37: Pull on the last loop to make it large enough to slip over whatever you want the toy to hang on and tie a knot around the end to prevent it from slipping. Trim the end.

Step 38: Secure the I-Cord to the ending tail of the jellyfish by knotting the two ends together.

Step 39: Tuck the tails through the center of the Gathered Removal Bind Off so they are in the center of the piece. Pull it so the knot is on the inside of the piece.

Step 40: Secure the knot with super glue to prevent it from pulling through. You can trim the ends or let them hang down as part of the toy.

Making Toys Fancier

Enhancements are a way of making toys more appealing, for both you and your cat. They aren't necessary, but they can be fun to do. And they are a great way to make each toy unique and special.

Bells

Bells are easily added to the beginning or the end of a toy because you can slip it on to the tail before tying the final knot. They are available in a multitude of sizes, but the 15mm ones seem to be the best size for the toys. Although, extra-large bells are an alternative option to a pom-pom for the center of the Flower Toy (p. 79). It can be difficult to get the yarn through the loop on the bell. Use the tip of your loom hook or an embroidery needle to push the yarn through. Wetting the end of the yarn may help. If the yarn end is too frayed, trim it. It takes effort, especially at first, so be patient. Some of my favorite places to add bells include at the end of the Small Twisty Door Hangers (p. 67), the Mouse's Tail (p. 82), and Q-Balls (p. 52).

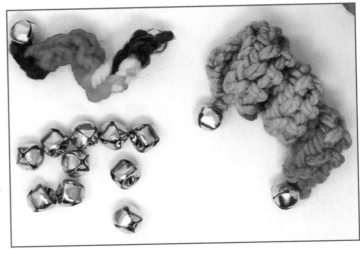

Beads

Beads with a large hole, such as pony beads, can be incorporated into your knitting if you plan ahead. Loop the beads onto the yarn before you start. It's best to put on more beads than you anticipate using as you can't add more once you begin. Knit the toy like normal until you are ready to add a bead. Then, when you want to add a bead, move it from the working yarn until it is close to the loom. Knit a stitch after it to secure the bead in place. My favorite toys to add beads include Balls (p. 22), I-Cord Toys (p. 41), and Q-Balls (p. 52).

Felt

Felt is safe to use as a decoration as it can be super glued on. Making the designs requires excellent cutting skills, or you could end up with shapes that look like drunk preschoolers made them. I don't use felt very often for that reason. But many craft stores sell precut felt shapes you can purchase as an alternative to making your own. The adhesive on these is not strong enough and you will need to reinforce it with super glue. Buying the letters allows you to personalize the Square Toy (p. 30), which is really the only toy in the book that has space for large felt shapes.

Fringe

Fringe is just tiny bits of yarn added to the end. My favorite way to add fringe is to leave the tail long instead of trimming it. This method works best when knitting with multiple strands. Another method is to cut pieces of yarn and knot them onto the toy. For your cat's safety, don't make the fringe too long. Long pieces, should they become detached, could be hazardous to your cat if he or she ingests it. Tie all extra pieces at least twice and secure the knots with super glue. Once the glue has dried, pull on each strand individually to test that they are securely attached.

Pompoms

Pompoms make great cat toys by themselves as well as great decorations. You can super glue the small ones on almost any of the toys.

Small white pompoms make great eyes. Use a permanent marker to add the pupil. Use plenty of glue to securely attach. Test that you used enough glue by attempting to pull it off once the glue has dried.

Googly Eyes

Googly eyes are another option, but one that I'm not overly excited about. In order for them to be safe, you should use small ones that are 4mm diameter. These are small enough that, should your cat manage to ingest them, wouldn't pose any real danger. (This was the opinion of a vet that I had asked.)

The problem with using eyes this size is that they are incredibly hard to glue on. And once glued on, they seemed too easy to pull off. But even worse, I didn't like how they looked. To look good, they need to be larger, but I don't feel the larger ones would be as safe as I would like.

Stitch Patterns and Purl Stitches

By combining knit and purl stitches you can create stitch patterns (often referred to simply as "loom stitches"). If you are interested in learning these patterns, knitting-forkittens.com offers some places you can learn them.

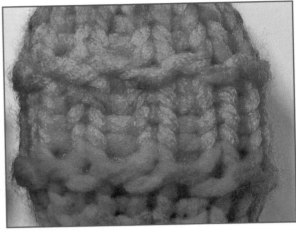

However, rows of purl stitches can be used to create interest in the toy without learning a complicated stitch pattern. If you repeatedly purl the same peg on a loom, it creates "ribbing." If you decide to do this, mark the pegs you want to purl with small rubber bands, bits of yarn or even a pencil mark. Otherwise, you could forget to switch stitches when you get to that peg.

If you add a row of purl stitches around the loom, you create a raised line of texture. Unfortunately, this also creates small openings in the knit fabric, so you are limited to what you use to stuff the toy.

Catnip

While it is not necessary to infuse toys with catnip, it is a nice bonus. Catnip (Nepeta cataria) is a member of the mint family that can cause cats to rub their heads and bodies on it, roll around and vocalize (amongst other behaviors). According to veterinarian Ramona Turner in *Scientific American*, only 70 to 80 percent of cats are affected by it. Kittens aren't affected by it until they are about 6 months old. A cat's response to catnip is also hereditary.

However, don't worry about your cats getting high. It's considered nonaddictive and harmless to cats. Typically, I take a bunch of toys and put them in a plastic bag with some catnip. I then leave them in there for a week before handing them out to cats. You can also create a catnip spray. Instructions are available on my website (basically you are making catnip tea and putting it in a spray bottle).

I've also stuffed catnip inside the toy itself (which is possible if you knit them with the u-wrap knit stitch). The e-wrap stitch, however, isn't tight enough and the catnip will leak out of the toy. The one drawback to adding catnip is the toy won't be washable.

Multiple Strands

The only difficult thing about knitting with multiple strands is that it can get confusing when trying to grab only the yarns of the existing loop to knit over. Keep the loops on the loom pushed down to provide space between the existing loop and the new loop.

Knitting with multiple strands should be done using several lighter strands, usually in the medium or lightweight. (See Yarn Weight on page 10 for more information.) I recommend doing this by adding a strand of light yarn to a strand of bulky yarn the first time. Although, with some yarns, the thinner yarn can get "lost" and you won't be able to see it.

To knit with multiple strands, grab the ends of each yarn, so they are parallel and create a slip knot. Then, with your new multi-strand yarn, knit like normal. Don't worry about keeping the strands parallel. It is too difficult and won't matter in the end.

Fuzzy Yarn

Using fuzzy yarn is almost essential once you get good at knitting mice. However, the longer the "fur" on the yarn, the more challenging it is to use. Also, because the yarn is usually too light or thin to use by itself, you need to combine it with a strand of regular yarn.

If using it for a toy with either the Drawstring Cast On, don't integrate the fuzzy strand until you start knitting the rows. The fuzziness can make it hard to pull the drawstring close. The same goes for the Gathered Removal Bind Off. Stop using the fuzzy strand before you begin binding off. It makes it difficult to pull the yarn through the loops to close them.

Before using any fuzzy yarn, test it by pulling on the hair to see if it comes apart easily. An alternative test would be to knit an I-Cord and toss it in the washing machine.

Switching Colors

Switching colors is the art of going from one skein of yarn to another. While there are plenty of ways to do this, I've found many of them can cause a gap in the knitting fabric. The method shown here does not do that. While it may not be the most elegant, it works well. It can't really be used on a flat piece, but works fine for toys like the Ball, Square and Mouse.

Step 1: Tie the end of Color 2 to the working yarn of Color 1. Slide the knot as close to the last peg knitted as you can.

Step 2: Knit the next peg with both yarns (Color 1 and Color 2). This will create two loops on the peg.

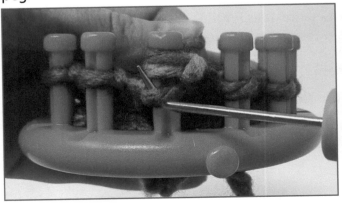

Step 3: Drop the Color 1 yarn and continue knitting with only Color 2 until you get to the pegs with 2 loops.

Step 4: When ready to knit the peg with 2 loops, knit both loops over the working yarn at the same time. Essentially, you are treating the two yarns as if they were one.

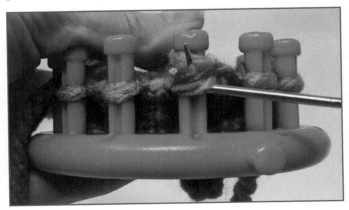

Ending the Color Switch

If Not Done Knitting with Color 1

Set Color 1 aside until you are ready to switch colors again. You will need to switch colors one peg after the peg where you switched. So if you switched on Peg 1, you will switch back on Peg 2. Trying to move the yarn to another peg can create a hole. When ready to switch back, pick up Color 1 and knit the next peg with Color 1 and Color 2. You will now follow Steps 1 through 4 above. Do not move to Step 5 until you are done knitting with one of the colors.

If Done Knitting with a Color

When you are done switching colors or don't plan on switching colors back, it's time to get rid of the extra skein of yarn. It doesn't matter if you do this with Color 1 or Color 2.

Step 5: Cut the working yarn from the skein leaving enough of a tail to tie a knot in it. Then, knot the tail to the working yarn of the other color to secure. Continue knitting with the remaining color.

Examples

Once you lean how to switch colors, you can use it in different ways. You can switch to one color, then switch back or never switch back. I've also switched back and forth between two colors to make stripes. Or if you're in patriotic mood, switch to a third color to get a red, white and blue toy. To get the "checkered" pattern seen in the toys on the right, you switch colors every other strand.

Glossary

The following are a list of loom knitting terms, definitions and/or abbreviations. Abbreviations were taken from Craft Yarn Council.

Anchor Peg: The peg on the side of the loom that is often used to secure, or "anchor," the yarn before you start a project. Not all looms have them.

Anchor Yarn: The yarn wrapped around the anchor peg, usually with a slip knot.

Bind Off (BO): Sometimes called "cast off," it is the method used to remove the securing the yarn and removing it from the loom.

Bound Off Edge: The finished end of your knitted piece.

Cast On (CO): The method used to start the yarn on the loom. One loop equals one stitch.

Cast On Edge: The starting end of your knitted piece.

Decrease: A method of reducing the number of stitches (pegs) on the loom.

Double Stitch (DS): When having 3 loops on a peg, knitting the bottom loop over the top two loops. A Double Stitch is used when creating Curly I-Cords.

Dropped Stitch: When a stitch comes off the peg. If not caught, it could unravel the entire stitch column.

Ending Tail: The yarn that exists after the knitting ends. It is the yarn after the last knit stitch.

Existing Loop: The loop of yarn on the peg. This loop is used to loop over the new loop to create a stitch.

Flat Knit: Refers either to a type of stitch or knitting a flat panel on a round loom. To flat knit, you reverse directions once you reach the end of your row of stitches.

Floats: When working with 2 or more colors of yarn, it refers to running the yarn across stitches on the wrong side of the fabric.

Gauge: The number of stitches in a horizontal span. For some patterns, gauge is extremely important, but not for the ones in this book.

Increase: A method of adding new stitches to a row.

Knit Off/Over (KO): Removing a wrap from a peg. This is usually done with the loom hook.

Knit Stitch: A knit stitch is the basic stitch that usually looks like a V in the knit fabric.

Knit: Technically, "knit" means to create a fabric with interlocking loops of wool. In this book, "knit" means to grasp the bottom loop over the top loop and off the beg.

Loom Hook: Used to move the loops on the loom. If you do a lot of loom knitting, I recommend getting an ergonomic one (it has a bigger handle) as it will be easier on your hand. I've learned you can never have too many loom hooks as they are easy to lose (check between the couch cushions).

Loom: The tool used to create weaves of yarn. Looms come in different varieties and sizes. This book uses a 12-peg round loom, also known as a flower loom. Peg Groove: an indention in the peg that makes knitting the yarn easier. Anchor Peg: The peg on the side of the loom. It may be used to hold the yarn at the start of the project or at any time during it.

Loop (lp): The yarn wrapped around the peg.

New Loop: The loop on the peg created with the working yarn that hasn't been knitted yet.

Purl Stitch: A basic stitch that looks like a line. It is the reverse of the knit stitch.

Rounds (rnd): When knitting on a round loom, rows are traditionally called rounds.

Row: Created either by going around the loom or by going from the starting peg to the ending peg.

Running Yarn: The yarn that goes between two pegs. It joins one stitch to another.

Seam: Joining two pieces together.

Skein of Yarn: Units of yarn have terms based on the shape they form when they are wound. A "ball" of yarn is one that is wrapped in a circle or ball shape, which is usually done by hand-winding it. Most yarn is sold in skeins, which is an oblong shape. For this reason, skein is also used to mean a unit of yarn, regardless of how it is wound. Other yarn forms include cake, hank, cone, and donut. In this book, skein or ball is used to refer as the basic unit of yarn.

Slip Knot: An adjustable loop. Every knit project begins with a slip knot.

Slip Stitch: Skipping a peg by running the working yarn either in front or behind a peg and working the next one.

Slipped Edge: Skipping the first peg of each row so the edge takes on a chain-like appearance.

Starting/Beginning Tail: The yarn that exists before the knitting begins. This is the yarn before the slip knot.

Stitches (st): The word stitch is used to describe two different things. In this book, it is used to refer to the basic way of creating new loops on a peg. There are five ways of doing this: e-wrap knit (EWK), u-wrap knit (UK), true knit (K), flat knit (FK), and purl (p). Stitches can also be used to refer to patterns created by combining knit and purl stitch. For example, the garter

stitch is created by alternating between rows of knit and purl stitches. For the purposes of this book, I will use what's called the stockinette stitch, or knit stitches all the way around.

Tail: Yarn at the end of the project that is not part of the knitting. It can be at the beginning or end of the project.

Tapestry Needle: A needle with a blunt tip and is larger than most sewing needles. You use it to tuck the ends of the yarn into your project. One is almost always included with any loom and can be purchased separately. They get lost easily (and at least my cats like to steal them), so I encourage you to purchase extras.

Waste Yarn: Scrap or leftover yarn. Keep small pieces of yarn to use in later projects.

Weave Ends: Hiding the yarn ends inside the project.

Working Yarn (WY): The yarn coming from the ball or skein. It is the section of yarn that you are using to create new stitches (in other words, working with).

Wrap: Looping the yarn around the peg. There are two basic types of wraps: e-wrap and u-wrap. E-Wrap (EW): Wrapping the working yarn completely around the peg. It gets its name because when done correctly, it looks like the cursive letter e. U-Wrap (UW): Wrapping the working yarn around the peg

Yarn Guide: A yarn guide is a tube that slips over the yarn. It is supposed to help you guide the yarn and (according to some sources) will help you create an even tension in the yarn.

Index

From the Author

Wow, you're actually reading this. I pretty much assumed no one would bother reading it. I hate writing them. I can write an entire book and then blank when I am forced to write a few paragraphs about the subject I am truly the expert on: myself.

So, instead I'll talk about how this book came to be. A little over a year ago I was in my favorite craft store and saw looms were half off. Like any good crafter with 100 unfinished projects I thought "I should loom knit." After making a few scarves and hats, I decided I wanted to make something for cats.

When not loom knitting or working, my life centers around cats. Yes, I am a crazy cat lady but it's crazy with a purpose. I foster cats and kittens. I have for several years. I usually foster kittens that are very sick. I have worked with some tremendous vets and learned skills that give them their best chance at survival. Sadly, not all survive, but most do.

And I thought it would be great to make cat toys that I could send with my fosters when they get adopted. But I couldn't find any cat toy patterns for the loom. Finally, I did find a video on how to make a ball, but of course it used a loom I didn't have: the 12-peg flower loom.

Yes, I went out and bought it. Once I learned how to make the ball, I tried to figure out other toys I could make. My goal was to have two or three toys. But one of the things I really wanted to make was a mouse. After a lot of trying and failing, I finally came up with a pattern that was easy to do and looked like a mouse.

But by this point, I had figured out dozens of other toys too. It was then that I decided to write this book. I had already three other books and a number of children's educational workbooks. It seemed easy. Unfortunately, my agent didn't feel she could represent it and the other agents and publishers I reached out to all wanted me to have a platform before they would consider it.

That's when I decided to publish it myself. I learned Adobe InDesign and Photoshop. I figured out how to take photos. I learned how to design a layout that made sense. It was a lot of work, but I'm very proud of the results.

I appreciate you taking a chance on this book. The profits from it will help me continue to foster and support open intake shelters in my area. I have a particular fondness for open intake shelters. After all, that was where I found Minx, the black cat featured in several of the photos. The kittens featured also came from an open-intake shelter in Camden county, New Jersey.

If you'd like to learn more, check out my website knittingforkittens.com. Until then, happy knitting!

Darcy Oordt

CPSIA information can be obtained
at www.ICGtesting.com
Printed in the USA
LVHW070023251120
672633LV00003B/33